MAXIMIZING LEAD GENERATION
The Complete Guide for B2B Marketers

Ruth P. Stevens

800 East 96th Street
Indianapolis, Indiana 46240 USA

Maximizing Lead Generation

Copyright © 2012 by Pearson Education, Inc.

All rights reserved. No part of this book shall be reproduced, stored in a retrieval system, or transmitted by any means, electronic, mechanical, photocopying, recording, or otherwise, without written permission from the publisher. No patent liability is assumed with respect to the use of the information contained herein. Although every precaution has been taken in the preparation of this book, the publisher and author assume no responsibility for errors or omissions. Nor is any liability assumed for damages resulting from the use of the information contained herein.

ISBN-13: 978-0-7897-4114-1
ISBN-10: 0-7897-4114-8

Library of Congress Cataloging-in-Publication Data:

Stevens, Ruth P. (Ruth Palmer)
  Maximizing lead generation : the complete guide for B2B marketers / Ruth P. Stevens.
      p. cm.
  ISBN-13: 978-0-7897-4114-1
  ISBN-10: 0-7897-4114-8
 1. Internet marketing. 2. Industrial marketing—Data processing.
3. Advertising, Industrial—Data processing. 4. Advertising campaigns—Data processing. I. Title.
  HF5415.1265.S745 201
  658.8'04—dc23
                                         2011020686
Printed in the United States of America

First Printing: July 2011

Trademarks

All terms mentioned in this book that are known to be trademarks or service marks have been appropriately capitalized. Que Publishing cannot attest to the accuracy of this information. Use of a term in this book should not be regarded as affecting the validity of any trademark or service mark.

Warning and Disclaimer

Every effort has been made to make this book as complete and as accurate as possible, but no warranty or fitness is implied. The information provided is on an "as is" basis. The author and the publisher shall have neither liability nor responsibility to any person or entity with respect to any loss or damages arising from the information contained in this book or from the use of the CD or programs accompanying it.

Bulk Sales

Que Publishing offers excellent discounts on this book when ordered in quantity for bulk purchases or special sales. For more information, please contact

    U.S. Corporate and Government Sales
    1-800-382-3419
    corpsales@pearsontechgroup.com

For sales outside of the U.S., please contact

    International Sales
    international@pearson.com

Editor-in-Chief
Greg Wiegand

Sr. Acquisitions Editor
Katherine Bull

Development Editor
Ginny Bess Munroe

Managing Editor
Kristy Hart

Project Editor
Anne Goebel

Indexer
Erika Millen

Proofreader
Sheri Cain

Publishing Coordinator
Cindy Teeters

Cover Designer
Anne Jones

Compositor
Nonie Ratcliff

Que Biz-Tech Editorial Board
Michael Brito
Jason Falls
Rebecca Lieb
Simon Salt
Peter Shankman

CONTENTS AT A GLANCE

1   The Case for Lead Generation 1

2   Campaign Planning: You Can't Leave It to Luck 19

3   The Marketing Database: Not Sexy, But Essential to Success 33

4   Campaign Development Best Practices 59

5   Campaign Media Selection 75

6   Campaign Execution 101

7   Response Planning and Management 123

8   Lead Qualification 139

9   Lead Nurturing 157

10 Metrics and Tracking 175

11 The Fast-Evolving Future of Lead Generation 191

    Index 199

TABLE OF CONTENTS

About the Author vii

Acknowledgments vii

We Want to Hear from You viii

1 The Case for Lead Generation 1

Defining Terms: What a Lead Is and What It Is Not 2

How Lead-Generation Campaigns Differ from Other Types
    of Marketing Communications 4

The Lead-Generation Process 6

Market Research for Lead Generation 10

Organizational Roles and Responsibilities for Lead Generation 12

Case Study in Lead-Generation Excellence: How Anritsu
    Reached Key Decision Makers with a Three-Touch Campaign 13

2 Campaign Planning: You Can't Leave It to Luck 19

Who? What? When? Where? Breaking Down the Buying Process 20

May I Have This Dance? 23

How Will You Know When You're There? 24

The Goldilocks School of Lead Flow Planning 25

Planning for Your Campaign Budget 28

3 The Marketing Database: Not Sexy, But Essential to Success 33

Data Sources and Types 34

Data Fields You Need for Lead Generation 46

Data Hygiene Best Practices 50

Database Analysis, Segmentation, and Modeling 54

4 Campaign Development Best Practices 59

Best Practice I: Research and Testing 60

Best Practice II: The New Importance of Content Marketing 66

Best Practice III: Marketing Automation 71

Case Study: When the Chips Were Down, Marketing Got Automated 73

5 Campaign Media Selection 75

B-to-B Lead Generation Media: The Top Five 77

Set the Stage for Lead Generation with PR 84

B-to-B Lead Generation Media: Three to Avoid 86

Using Web 2.0 for Lead Generation 88

How to Select the Right Media Mix 92

Mixing It Up: Multiple Media 93

6 Campaign Execution 101

Campaign Target Selection: Finding the Winning Combination 102

Seven Steps to Successful Lead-Generation Creative 106

How to Develop Offers They Can't Refuse 110

Getting the Best Work from an Agency or Creative Freelancers 118

7 Response Planning and Management 123

Response Management Step-by-Step 124

Six Strategies to Capture the Response Data You Need 124

The All-Important Landing Page 126

Why Responses Are Often Mishandled 131

Inquiry Fulfillment: The Beginning of a Beautiful Relationship 132

Six Rules of Fullfillment 134

8 Lead Qualification 139

Setting Qualification Criteria: Can't Beat BANT 140

What to Ask and When to Ask It 141

Need for Speed: Moving Qualified Leads into the Pipeline 142

Lead-Ranking Strategies 145

Qualifying Leads at a Trade Show or Event 150

Marketing Checkup for Telephone-Based Lead Generation
and Qualification 151

The Whos and Hows of the Handoff 153

9   Lead Nurturing **157**

    A Marketing Function with a Big Sales Benefit 158

    The Lead-Nurturing Process, Step by Step 159

    Nurturing Best Practices 161

    Case Study: How a Comprehensive Rethinking of Lead Generation
       and Management Strategy Improved Lead-Nurturing Response
       Rates and Lowered Costs 167

10   Metrics and Tracking **175**

    Response Rate 176

    Cost Per Lead 179

    Inquiry-to-Lead Conversion Rate 181

    Lead-to-Sales Conversion Rates 182

    Expense-to-Revenue Ratio (E:R) 183

    Seven Techniques for Tracking Leads to Closure 185

    When a Lead Doesn't Close 190

11   The Fast-Evolving Future of Lead Generation **191**

    1. More and Better Marketing Automation 192

    2. Sales and Marketing Will Finally Get on the Same Page 192

    3. New Data Sources for Prospecting 193

    4. Social Media Will Get Real for Lead Generation 193

    5. Affinity Marketing Will Come to B-to-B 194

    6. Face-to-Face Events Will Resume Their Importance 194

    7. New Ways to Nurture 195

    8. Ever-Evolving Customer Behavior 196

    9. More and Better Video 196

    10. Mobile Will Happen 197

Index **199**

About the Author

Ruth P. Stevens consults on customer acquisition and retention, and she teaches marketing at Columbia Business School. She is past chair of the DMA Business-to-Business Council, and past president of the Direct Marketing Club of New York. Crain's *BtoB* magazine named Ruth one of the 100 Most Influential People in Business Marketing, and the Sales Lead Management Association listed her as one of 20 Women to Watch in lead management. She is the author of *Trade Show and Event Marketing*, and she has been a columnist and feature writer for *DMNews, DIRECT*, and *EXPO* magazines. Ruth serves as a director of Edmund Optics, Inc. She has held senior marketing positions at Time Warner, Ziff-Davis, and IBM and holds an MBA from Columbia University. Reach her at ruth@ruthstevens.com.

Acknowledgments

My sincere thanks go to the many people and companies who supported this book with ideas, interviews, statistics, and general good will. Among the individuals are Andrew Drefahl, Ann Fatino, Ardath Albee, Bernice Grossman, Bill Flatley, Bill Hebel, Bill Vorias, Bob Bly, Bob Burk, Bob Hacker, Cesar Correia, Cyndi Greenglass, Dave Laverty, David Azulay, David Gaudreau, Denise Olivares, Gottfried Sehringer, Hugh McFarlane, Jan Wallen, Jim Lenskold, Jim Obermayer, Joe Pulizzi, John Hasbrouck, John Price, Karen Breen Vogel, Katherine VanDiepen, Larry Chase, Laurie Beasley, Lee Marc Stein, Leonard Bronfeld, Linda Tenenbaum, Mark Klein, Marten G. van Pelt, Mary Brandon, Michael A. Brown, Michael Veit, Mike Chaplo, Mike Schultz, Paul Gillin, Reggie Brady, Richard N. Tooker, Richard Vancil, Rob Lail, Robert Lesser, Robert Reneau, Russell Kern, Sean Shea, Spyro Kourtis, Stephen D. Armstrong, Steven R. Lett, Susanne Sicilian, T.J. Gillett, Ted Birkhahn, Tom Judge, and Valerie Mason Cunningham.

Among the companies and organizations are the Content Marketing Institute, The Direct Marketing Association, GlobalSpec, Marketing Sherpa, MarketingProfs, the Sales Lead Management Association, and the Hacker Group.

I also thank the Pearson editorial team, Katherine Bull, Ginny Munroe, and Anne Goebel, for their excellent guidance.

In particular, I want to thank Steve Gershik, who generously read the book in manuscript form and provided much insight and wisdom, and Jackie Ball of WriteB2B, who tirelessly helped shape the manuscript and added enormous value to the project.

—R. P. S.

We Want to Hear from You!

As the reader of this book, *you* are our most important critic and commentator. We value your opinion and want to know what we're doing right, what we could do better, what areas you'd like to see us publish in, and any other words of wisdom you're willing to pass our way.

As Editor-in-Chief for Que Publishing, I welcome your comments. You can email or write me directly to let me know what you did or didn't like about this book—as well as what we can do to make our books better.

Please note that I cannot help you with technical problems related to the topic of this book. We do have a User Services group, however, where I will forward specific technical questions related to the book.

When you write, please be sure to include this book's title and author as well as your name, email address, and phone number. I will carefully review your comments and share them with the author and editors who worked on the book.

Email: feedback@quepublishing.com

Mail: Greg Wiegand
         Editor-in-Chief
         Que Publishing
         800 East 96th Street
         Indianapolis, IN 46240 USA

For more information about this book or another Que Publishing title, visit our web-site at www.quepublishing.com. Type the ISBN (excluding hyphens) or the title of a book in the Search field to find the page you're looking for.

1

The Case for Lead Generation

Lead generation involves identifying prospective customers and qualifying their likelihood to buy in advance of making a sales call. In short, it's about motivating prospects to raise their hands.

Lead generation is the single most important objective of any business-to-business (B-to-B) marketing department. Other objectives, such as brand building, brand stewardship, public relations, and corporate communications are also on the list, to be sure. But, providing a sales force with a steady stream of qualified leads is job one.

When asked, senior marketing executives back this up. In a 2010 study, Marketing Sherpa asked chief marketing officers (CMOs) about the challenges they face. The top answer was "generating high-quality leads," named by 76 percents of respondents. Tellingly, the 76 percent response rate for this answer was up from 69 percent the prior year, so it appears that CMOs are increasingly under pressure in the lead-generation arena.

Furthermore, the other issues keeping CMOs up at night are also heavily about leads. In Table 1.1, you can see the survey results in detail.

Table 1.1 CMO Challenges	
Which of the following marketing challenges are currently most pertinent to your organization?	**Percent of respondents, 2010**
Generating high-quality leads	76%
Marketing to a growing number of people involved in the buying process	45%
Generating a high volume of leads	39%
Marketing to a lengthening sales cycle	39%
Generating public relations "buzz"	39%
Generating perceived value in "cutting edge" product benefits	37%
Competing in lead generation across multiple media	32%

Source: Marketing Sherpa B-to-B Benchmark Survey

So, it's fair to conclude that lead generation is critically important to business marketers. But, despite the importance of leads, the term "lead" is often misunderstood.

Defining Terms: What a Lead Is and What It Is Not

A *lead* is a prospect that has some level of potential of becoming a customer. We need to distinguish a lead from a business inquiry or from a mere list of names, with which leads are commonly confused. Mailing lists or contact lists of business prospects are often presented as "lead lists," a misnomer that generates not only confusion but even ill will in the world of business marketing. A passive list of prospects (or, more appropriately, suspects) does not deserve to be called a list of leads.

The same holds true for inquirers. Simply because someone has expressed a modicum of interest in your product or your company does not mean that person or that company is ready, willing, or able to buy. But an inquirer has plenty of value. You can continue to communicate, nurture that interest, and keep a relationship going until a sale is imminent.

Marketers must deliver a lead to the sales team only when the lead is truly qualified, and they must do so by criteria developed in consultation with the sales force. Consistent delivery of qualified leads that convert satisfyingly to sales and meet sales quotas—that is the hallmark of successful B-to-B lead generation.

The process of lead generation is fairly straightforward; however, it does involve a long and somewhat complex series of steps, beginning with a series of outbound and inbound contacts to generate the inquiry and qualify it, to handing the lead to the sales organization, and then tracking the lead through conversion to sales revenue.

The secret to success is in a focus on business rules and processes, as boring as that might sound. Lead generation and management are not the glamorous creative sides of marketing. They are more about developing the rules, refining them, testing, tracking them, and continuous improvement. This is not to say creativity cannot have impact. It can.

 Tip

The company with the best lead-generation process, executed consistently, is the one with the true competitive advantage.

Many parties are involved in the process, both internal to the company and external. Each has a role and each has a share in the credit for the results. To be successful in this kind of business environment, marketers must focus on fairly elaborate planning and process development, regular consultation with sales, disciplined measurements and analysis, and constant communication with everyone.

There is a certain amount of disagreement about the "right" meaning of various terms in lead generation. In fact, there is no right or wrong. Companies and cultures tend to create their own definitions, which are passed down internally from management generation to generation. Usage also varies from industry to industry. Following are the definitions of terms as they are used in this book:

- **Prospect.** An individual or company that is likely to need your product or services, but has not bought from you yet.

- **Customer.** An individual or company that has made a purchase from you.

- **Inquiry.** The first inbound contact from a prospective customer. It might come in "over the transom" or, more likely, from a campaign. The inquiry might also come from a current customer who seeks a refill, a replacement, an upgrade, or a new product.

- **Response rate.** The rate at which prospects or customers respond to an outbound campaign. It is calculated by dividing the number of responses by the number of prospects promoted. After they are received, the responses are called inquiries.

- **Lead (also called qualified lead).** An inquiry that has met the agreed-upon qualification criteria, such as having the right budget, decision-making authority, need for the product or service, and readiness to make the purchase in a suitable amount of time. After an inquiry has become a qualified lead, it is ready to be worked by a sales person.

- **Qualification.** The process by which you establish whether the inquiry is qualified to become a lead.

- **Qualification rate.** The rate at which inquiries migrate to qualified leads. It is calculated by dividing the number of qualified leads during a period, or from a particular campaign, by the number of inquiries in the period or from the campaign.

- **Nurturing.** The process of moving an unqualified inquiry to the point where it becomes qualified. Some inquiries qualify right away. Many, however, need some nurturing via outbound communications until the prospect is entirely ready to be contacted by a sales person.

- **Conversion.** When a lead becomes a sale.

- **Closed lead.** A lead that has converted into a sale.

- **Conversion rate.** The rate at which qualified leads convert to sales. It is calculated by dividing the number of closed leads by the number of qualified leads delivered to the sales force.

How Lead-Generation Campaigns Differ from Other Types of Marketing Communications

Lead generation is a different animal from general advertising or marketing communications. The biggest difference is that lead generation relies on direct marketing, also known as direct-response marketing communications. Direct marketing comprises a set of marketing tools, approaches, and activities that are targeted, measurable, and driven by return-on-investment (ROI) considerations. But the key difference is that direct marketing's goal is to motivate an action. The action can be anything from a click, to a phone call, to a store visit—whatever the goal of the marketer is.

Based on customer information captured and maintained in a database and using a variety of analytical and communications techniques, direct marketing provides the underpinnings of some of today's most effective marketing approaches. These approaches include e-commerce, data mining, customer relationship management (CRM), and integrated marketing communications. But the major contribution that direct marketing makes to the business marketing equation is generating leads for a sales force, whether a field sales team, inside sales, or an outside sales resource like a distribution channel partner or representative.

B-TO-B DIRECT MARKETING IS BIG BUSINESS

The Direct Marketing Association publishes some interesting statistics on the size and value of direct marketing in business markets. Consider these from *The DMA 2010 Statistical Fact Book*:

- B-to-B direct marketing spending in all media channels in 2010 was $74.6 billion.

- Spending growth rate (CAGR) between 2009 and 2014 is expected to be 4.9 percent for B-to-B, compared to only 4 percent for the consumer direct marketing spend.

- B-to-B sales driven by direct marketing in 2010 represented $786 billion.

- Sales growth CAGR in 2009 to 2014 is estimated at 5.4 percent, compared to 4.9 percent in consumer.

- An estimated 3.9 million people were employed in B-to-B direct marketing in the U.S. in 2009. This is big business, in every sense of the word.

Besides direct-response marketing, there are two additional ways that lead generation is different from other forms of marketing communications. For one thing, lead generation is about quality versus quantity. Sales people are an expensive resource for a company. The job of lead generation is to make them more productive. So, it's not about a wide reach and a lot of volume. In fact, fewer, better leads trump more, lower quality leads every time.

Second, lead generation tends to be down there on the ground. It's about helping sales, driving results in the field, and connecting to revenue. Often, lead generation is part of a function called field marketing and is seen as a more tactical set of activities than the strategic marketing that goes on in corporate communications, in brand building, and public relations. Some lead generators get miffed about their relatively tactical role, feeling that they are somehow viewed as lesser beings than the general marketers who think about so-called bigger picture marketing. This is a subject of ongoing debate in the B-to-B world. In my view, however, anything that is the primary occupation of 76 percent of CMOs is certainly worth a lot of respect.

The Lead-Generation Process

Lead generation is, frankly, more a science than an art. It is based on process, best practices, and continuous testing and improvement. As noted, the company with the best process wins. Smart marketers focus on each step in the process, looking for ways to make it more efficient. The end result pays off in lower costs and higher conversion rates to sales. The following sections describe the steps, in planning order, but not necessarily in order of importance (they are all important). Each of these process steps is discussed in detail in this book.

Inquiry Generation

Reaching out to prospects and generating an initial response begins the process. To break inquiry generation down, you can look at it, too, as a series of steps:

1. **Set campaign objectives.** Most lead-generation campaigns select from the following objectives:

    - The number of leads expected.

    - The degree of qualification.

    - The time frame during which they will arrive.

    - The cost per lead.

    - Lead-to-sales conversion ratio.

    - Revenue per lead.

    - Campaign ROI or expense-to-revenue ratio.

    - Choose one primary and no more than two secondary objectives, and make them very specific.

2. **Analyze and select campaign targets.** The tighter your targeting, the higher your response is likely to be. Current customers, of course, respond better than cold prospects. In fact, some companies find that much of their lead-generation work involves finding new opportunities in accounts they already have relationships with. So, it's not cold prospecting, but it's still an effort to generate business for new products, new buyer groups, or additional divisions or business units in the account. That said, most B-to-B marketers focus on entirely new accounts for their lead-generation programs.

3. **Select campaign media.** For generating leads among new prospects, the best choices are SEM, telemarketing, and direct mail for ongoing

campaign work. Trade shows, web-based lead generation, and referral marketing programs can also be effective. Among inquirers and current customers, you will find telephone and email most productive, telephone being more intrusive and email being the less expensive option.

4. **Develop a message platform.** The platform is the key benefit that appeals to the target audience. Your response improves if you keep the message simple and focus on a single benefit.

5. **Develop a campaign offer.** This subject is discussed in detail in Chapter 6, "Campaign Execution." For now, suffice it to say that the purpose of the offer is to motivate the target prospect to respond with an indication of interest in your product or service. Don't be fooled into thinking that you can get away without a motivating offer of some sort. You can't.

6. **Create communications.** Unlike general advertising communications, the copy is the most important element of your lead generation creative treatment, so use a professional direct-response copywriter who has B-to-B experience.

7. **Plan fulfillment materials.** Speed is of the essence. Studies show that the faster the fulfillment materials are received, the more likely the lead is to be qualified. The need is still fresh, and competitors are less likely to be in the way. As a rule of thumb, inquiries should be fulfilled no later than 24 hours after receipt, if using printed materials, and instantaneously if using a landing page with downloadable materials.

Response Planning

Planning for response management is a critical and sometimes sorely neglected part of preparing a lead-generation campaign. You will not regret the effort you put into ensuring your prospects' responses are properly handled and tracked. In fact, some would argue that if this work is not done right, you are throwing your marketing investments out the window.

Start response planning early in the campaign-development process. Make sure you have a unique code that identifies responses from every outbound communication. This can be a priority code, a special toll-free number, an operator's name, a unique URL, anything. Offer multiple response media, including landing page, phone, business reply card (BRC), fax, and email. Don't be shy about including qualification questions on your reply form or your inbound-phone scripts. Response planning is covered in detail in Chapter 7, "Response Planning and Management."

Response Capture

The response capture process works only if it's designed by the people who manage the inbound media through which the response arrives. Put together a cross-functional team. Then, consider the best strategy for each medium. Ensure electronic inquiries from email and landing pages are acted on immediately. Log the inquiries into a database and match the names against prior contacts to avoid duplicates.

Internal processes must be set up in advance to capture and record the key codes for later analysis. Make sure the teams handling the responses—whether they are internal call centers or outsourced fulfillment companies—are well trained and motivated to capture as many codes as possible. Despite your best efforts, a certain amount of inbound responses inevitably go uncaptured. The best way to handle them for analysis is to separate the uncoded responses and analyze the trackable responses on their own. Response capture is discussed in detail in Chapter 7.

Inquiry Fulfillment

Most B-to-B inquiries ask for more information, so give it to them. Make your responses snappy. Match the fulfillment material to the need and the value of the prospect.

Today, the big news in inquiry fulfillment is the new science of "content marketing," which is sweeping the B-to-B marketing world. Understanding that business buyers research the solutions to business problems online, long before they call in a salesperson to help them, marketers create vast libraries of so-called "content assets." These are available to educate and inform customers and prospects, and to demonstrate thought leadership among influential parties in their particular fields. These assets make excellent fodder for lead generation, as offers to motivate response, as content for effective lead nurturing to help move prospects along their buying journeys, and to stay in touch and deepen relationships with current customers. The fascinating new subject of content marketing is discussed in Chapter 4, "Campaign Development Best Practices."

Inquiry Qualification

Nothing is more important than correctly qualifying sales leads before they are delivered to the sales people. It is a frequent misunderstanding on the part of marketers that lead volume is the objective. In fact, it is quality that counts. The objective is to generate enough qualified leads so that each sales territory is optimally busy, productive, and fulfilling its quota. More is not necessarily better. Delivering too many leads can be as wasteful as delivering too few. Delivering qualified leads is what provides real leverage to that expense and constrained resource: the sales force.

Most inquiries require additional qualification before they are ready for handoff to sales. The secret to qualification is involvement of the sales team in setting qualification criteria. A good way to elicit an idea of the ideal prospect is to ask a few sales managers and sales reps to describe their ideal prospect, in terms of type of company, job role, and needs. Some will tell you they want to be given every response that comes in from their territory. But your job is to deliver to them only leads that are ready to take up their valuable time. Lead qualification and how to set qualification criteria are discussed in Chapter 8, "Lead Qualification."

Lead Nurturing

When an inquiry is only partially qualified and does not make the grade of readiness for the sales team, it needs to be nurtured in a process that is called *incubation* or *lead development*. Nurturing involves a series of communications intended to build trust and awareness, and keep a relationship going until the prospect is ready to buy. You can use a variety of tactics, from newsletters, to surveys, to white papers, to birthday cards.

Sources of leads that require nurturing include

- **Partially qualified inquiries.** They are not ready to deliver to sales, according to the predefined qualification criteria.

- **Leads returned by the sales team.** Frequently, a presumably qualified lead turns out to require further nurturing. The contact might have changed jobs, or the business need might have changed. So, the sales people return the lead to marketing for further follow-up.

The nurturing process can be fast or slow—or endless. Some prospects never get the budget, or their needs change, or they buy from a competitor. This can be discouraging. But, just remind yourself that somewhere around half of all business inquiries eventually result in a sale—for someone, anyway—so you can find the energy and the funding to put in place a robust and effective nurturing process. This entire subject is discussed in Chapter 9, "Lead Nurturing."

Lead Tracking

Let's not forget the process of closing the marketing loop to attribute a closed sale to a marketing campaign. Business marketers operating in a multichannel world are continually challenged by problems in measuring the results of their lead-generation campaigns. Without solid measurements, it's hard to demonstrate the value of marketing, not to mention justify the budgets. But, the most important reason for careful measurement is to give you the tools to refine campaign tactics and improve results next time.

When multiple people and functions are involved at various stages of the lead-generation and conversion process, evaluating the contribution of each element can be impossible. Most B-to-B lead-generation campaigns rely on a combination of activity-based metrics, such as cost per lead, and results-based metrics, such as lead-to-sales conversion rates, revenue, and ROI. A variety of tools to help you close the loop between a lead-generation campaign and an eventual sale are presented in Chapter 10, "Metrics and Tracking."

Market Research for Lead Generation

In the spirit of ready, aim, fire, lead generation is much improved with the help of advance research, like any marketing activity. Perhaps the most essential pre-campaign research you can do is about selecting targets. In the long term and short term, some research can have a positive impact on your lead-generation results.

Traditionally, research for sales lead generation was done at a business library, by poring through directories of companies, professional associations, and trade publications. The going was slow, and the data likely to be stale.

These days, the primary tool is the Internet, which has become the first line of attack for researchers of all types. The simplest, and perhaps most popular, technique is a simple Google search. But the results are not going to be useful unless you already have a clear idea of who you want to find.

Say, for example, you sell ERP software to the apparel industry. Your objective is to find apparel manufacturers who want to install new software or upgrade their existing systems. A Google search for "apparel manufacturers" brings up nearly 8 million hits. Odd, because a quick trip to the Bureau of Labor Statistics (www.bls.gov) reveals that there are only 16,000 people employed in managerial roles in this industry nationwide. It makes no sense to begin trolling through even the first 100 of those hits.

An alternative is to buy an industry directory that is sold over the Internet. The Directory of Brand Name Apparel Manufacturers (www.fashiondex.com), for example, sells a hard copy listing of the company contacts at 2,800 brands in 65 apparel categories for $115. We know that there are more than 2,800 companies in this industry, and a print-based directory will no doubt include a high percent of outdated content.

Ideal is an online research resource that allows you to sort companies and individual contacts according to the variables that typically drive sales targeting strategies:

- Industry (or SIC or NAICS codes)
- Company size (whether revenue or number of employees)
- Geographic location
- Title or job function

Once the right companies are identified, then it's a matter of selecting the right individuals. Some online resources allow you to search not only by job function, but also by variables such as

- Age
- Business biography or background
- Salary or total compensation
- Name

Then, of course, you want to access full contact information so that the initial conversation can begin.

A number of useful strategies for identifying high-potential prospects and refining the search have been developed by leading companies over the years. Here are three of the best approaches:

- To get a sense of the highest potential prospects for your product or service, use the "look-alike" method. Review the characteristics of your best customers, and identify the lookalikes in the universe of prospects. For example, if your top accounts are apparel manufacturers in New York and California, with sales of $25 million to $50 million annually, you will do well by starting with that demographic target.

- Examine the buying process in your target industry. If ERP software purchases are a joint decision between the IT and finance departments, then you will want to select multiple contacts at the apparel firms, with titles like CFO and CIO, as well as the usual CEO.

- Keep in mind that a name selected based on demographic targeting, no matter how refined, is unlikely to comprise a fully qualified sales lead. These contacts will be yours to include in your lead-generation campaign, to motivate them to raise their hands, and then to assess the quality of the prospect against such qualification criteria as product interest, whether a budget is available, the purchasing authority of the prospect, and the urgency of the need for your product or service.

Organizational Roles and Responsibilities for Lead Generation

Lead generation is a relatively complex process involving not only the marketing function, but many other areas of a company. So, there is always going to be some confusion about who should do what to whom. Whatever you do, clarify roles early on during the planning process; it can save much pain later.

Each organization should make its own decisions, but following are some suggested guidelines for roles and responsibilities. There is some overlap, of course. Table 1.2 suggests what job function typically takes the lead on each element of lead-generation tools and processes.

Table 1.2   Lead-Generation Roles and Responsibilities by Function

Function	Role and Responsibilities
Marketing	Strategic planning, market analysis and targeting, budgeting, setting sales, and marketing objectives
Marketing communications	Advertising and PR for building brand awareness
Direct marketing	Lead generation, lead qualification, nurturing, and tracking
Database marketing	Marketing database management, data analysis, and list selection
Event marketing	Trade show, proprietary event execution, and data capture
Sales force	Lead conversion to sales and reporting on lead status
Resellers/distributors	Lead conversion to sales and reporting on lead status
Web marketing	Website management and landing page management
IT	Install software tools and tech support

Following are a few particular caveats for roles and responsibilities:

- Do not allow the lead management (qualification, nurturing, and tracking) function to rest with the sales team. Sales may want to make a strong case for controlling this function. But ultimately, lead management belongs in marketing. Sales resources are highly skilled and well paid. They need to be focused on selling.

- Marketing needs to have a key role in managing the marketing database and the campaign software tools. In most companies, IT has ultimate responsibility for these tools, but they need to recognize the critical role marketing plays in specifying, using, and benefiting from them.

Case Study in Lead-Generation Excellence: How Anritsu Reached Key Decision Makers with a Three-Touch Campaign

To whet your appetite for how powerfully lead-generation programs can help drive your business success, enjoy the case of Anritsu, who cleverly figured out how to find and attract wireless industry engineers to express interest in learning more about a new handheld instrument for testing cellular base station transmitters.

Anritsu, a leader in test and measurement equipment for the wireless industry, had a problem getting through to its target audience for the company's handheld BTS Master Base Station Analyzer. The decision makers their sales team coveted were hard-to-reach engineers who spent most of their time in the field. Historically, these professionals had responded poorly to Anritsu's email and direct mail campaigns, converting from prospect to sales lead at a rate of only 2 percent. Anritsu's marketers needed a way to engage the other 98 percent. After they had the prospects' undivided attention, their job would be to convince them that Anritsu's instrument was faster, more accurate, and more compact than its competitors'.

Anritsu's director of marketing communications, Katherine Van Diepen, engaged Beasley Direct Marketing Inc. and Direct Marketing Partners to produce a multi-touch, door-opener campaign. The program's objectives were to

- Penetrate the sales team's wish list, comprising about 1,500 key customer targets at the four top wireless carriers in the U.S.

- Engage key decision makers.

- Set appointments for in-person demos.

- Enhance and validate the target database for future efforts.

- Track results and demonstrate a positive ROI.

Over the course of three months, the program's developers planned to achieve their objectives with three highly targeted touches. The first touch was a personalized, dimensional direct mail piece sent with a box replicating the product's compact size and picturing its actual controls on the outside, as shown in Figure 1.1. Respondents were invited to visit a personalized landing page (see Figure 1.2), which was pre-populated with the prospect's contact information. A business reply card (BRC), pictured in Figure 1.3, also came inside the box along with a brochure.

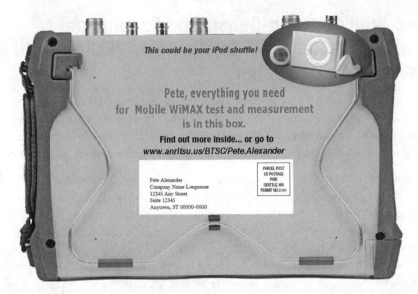

Figure 1.1 The dimensional mail's packaging shows a life-size replica of the instrument itself, along with a highly attractive offer, a personalized technical message, and personalized URL response vehicle.
Illustration used with permission from Anritsu Corporation.

The second touch was a personalized email to the same target audience. The email, shown in Figure 1.4, was intended to drive responders to a PURL.

A third touch, in the form of a personalized teleprospecting call to responders and nonresponders, came a day or two after the email.

The call to action for all three touch points were the same: to set an appointment for an in-person demonstration of the base station analyzer. A free iPod Shuffle (preloaded with Anritsu's datasheets and collateral) would be the incentive offer. The results? Wow!

To say the program was successful is a mammoth understatement. The campaign improved the response rate by a staggering 425 percent over prior campaigns and delivered seven-digit sales revenues. An enviable 7 percent of total targets visited the landing page, and 4 percent filled out the response form. A full 49 percent of prospects contacted by telephone emerged as qualified leads. At last tally, the return on marketing investment (revenue to expense ratio) was 41 to 1.

It doesn't stop there. In addition to exceeding sales-ready lead targets, the program gave Anritsu a model to drive revenue from hard-to-engage accounts. It's no small wonder that the program earned an Echo Award from the Direct Marketing Association in the highly competitive Information Technology category.

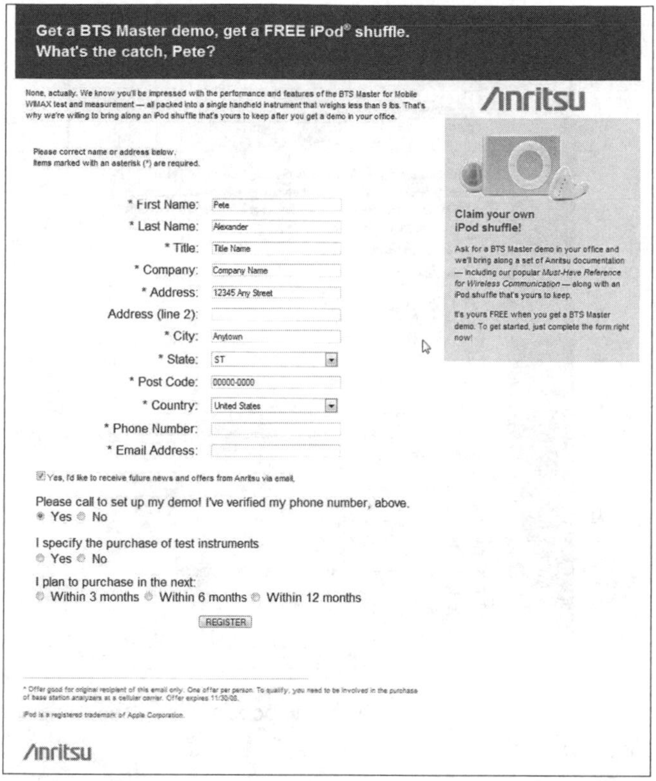

Figure 1.2   The personalized landing page (PURL) response form was pre-populated with the respondent's contact information; it included a few key qualifying questions, and it resold the iPod Shuffle offer.

The secrets to the success of this campaign:

- A clear understanding of the target market, their motivations, and their buying process

- Multiple touches through proven media channels, deployed to capture the maximum penetration of a relatively narrow segment

- A powerful set of benefits and a compelling offer

- Strong focus on metrics, tracking the performance on each touch, not only response but qualification rates, and conversion to sales

In short, this campaign took advantage of proven best practices in B-to-B lead generation today. So, now, on to the rest of this book, where you can learn these practices and principles for yourself.

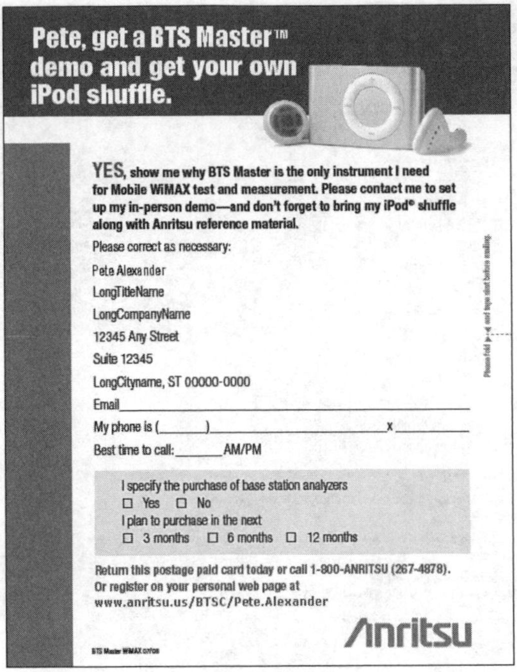

Pete, get a BTS Master™ demo and get your own iPod shuffle.

YES, show me why BTS Master is the only instrument I need for Mobile WiMAX test and measurement. Please contact me to set up my in-person demo—and don't forget to bring my iPod® shuffle along with Anritsu reference material.

Please correct as necessary:

Pete Alexander
LongTitleName
LongCompanyName
12345 Any Street
Suite 12345
LongCityname, ST 00000-0000

Email______________________________________

My phone is (______)______________________x_________

Best time to call:_______AM/PM

I specify the purchase of base station analyzers
☐ Yes ☐ No
I plan to purchase in the next
☐ 3 months ☐ 6 months ☐ 12 months

Return this postage paid card today or call 1-800-ANRITSU (267-4878). Or register on your personal web page at www.anritsu.us/BTSC/Pete.Alexander

Anritsu

Figure 1.3 The printed reply form inside the box employed the same strategies as the web-based form to stimulate response.

Figure 1.4   The follow-up email, timed to arrive shortly after the dimensional mail, resells the key product benefits and the compelling offer.

2

Campaign Planning: You Can't Leave It to Luck

Like uninvited guests, sometimes leads appear at your door out of the blue. They may be prospects who have been referred by a current customer or they may have discovered your company through research. They may be current customers looking for a product or service upgrade. Whoever they are, unlike most uninvited guests, they deserve the warmest welcome. You can depend on them to behave beautifully, usually converting to sales with minimal cost and effort on your part. The only thing wrong with these so-called over-the-transom leads is that there aren't enough of them.

You can—and should—increase your company's potential to attract unsolicited leads by offering superior product quality and exceptional customer service, but peering out the window and hoping someone will drop by is not a strategy for a healthy, growing business. You need to keep sending out invitations, deliberately generating leads through outbound campaigns.

Lead-generation campaigns take careful planning because there are many factors involved. Where do you start? You begin by taking off your marketer's hat and getting inside the head of your customers and prospects—more precisely, you get inside their buying processes. You need to analyze every step in the process in every market segment you want to target.

Who? What? When? Where? Breaking Down the Buying Process

Start your analysis by cribbing the "W" page from a reporter's notebook. Ask:

- Who is the buyer—one person or a committee?
- What information do the buyers need to make their decision?
- When do they buy, and how long is their buying cycle?
- Where do they buy?

Knowing the answers is essential to every element of your campaigning process, from selecting the most effective media, to crafting the right creative approaches, to assembling the necessary collateral materials. Here are some examples of why this detailed knowledge is crucial:

- **Who.** Especially for high-ticket items, companies often put together a task force comprising individuals from different departments. A campaign that targets a committee faces the challenge of reaching all members whose jobs and roles relative to the purchase are widely diverse. A recent study from Marketing Sherpa found that for a purchase over $25,000, buying committees average 21 members in larger companies (over 1,000 employees).

- **What.** Most companies do extensive product research to determine their needs, review the options available, and assess the best way to solve their problem. They want information, and lots of it, before they make a purchase. Your campaign materials should be information-rich, with numerous easy, convenient ways for people to contact you with questions or to request more information. And don't forget to have the personnel available to answer those questions when they come. This is why content marketing has become so important in B-to-B settings (see Chapter 4, "Campaign Development Best Practices").

- **When.** If you know a company sends out requests for bids once a month, you can schedule a monthly outbound call to stay on top of due dates, submission requirements, contacts, and other procedural details.

- **Where.** Does each branch of a company have its own, autonomous purchasing department, or is buying centralized at headquarters or some other site? Or, perhaps the decision making happens at one location and the purchase order is issued from another. You need to know what happens where.

Although this can get complicated, buying processes do tend to be fairly similar by company size and within industries, which can reduce the complexity of your analysis. After you complete this detailed analysis, you can map your campaigning and selling processes to the buying process in each targeted segment. You'll be able to anticipate the buyer's next moves and be ready with the right materials or resources to influence the purchasing decision every step of the way.

KEY PLAYERS IN THE PURCHASE DECISION

It's not uncommon for numerous individuals to be involved in the buying process, especially in larger companies. Marketing Sherpa's Business Technology Buyers Survey showed in 2007 that as many as 21 parties are involved in a $25k+ purchase decision at companies with more than 1,000 employees. Marketers often refer to this "gang of 21" as the *buying circle.* It's our job to identify the members of this circle, determine their roles in the purchase decision, and then figure out how to influence them in our favor.

Each of the parties in the buying circle has a different agenda, so you must customize your approach to each. For example, if I am selling custom-engineered turbine generator sets to harness waste steam from industrial boilers to convert it to electricity, I have a buying circle that looks like this:

- The plant manager, who plays the role of "user" in the buying circle, is concerned with questions such as, "How will this disrupt my plant?" and "Will it make me look good?"

- The corporate energy executive, the influencer, wants to see specifics about the environmental benefits of the project.

- To the VP of manufacturing operations, the decision maker, it's all about the ROI compared to other capital investment options.

- The plant engineer is the specifier, and wants to know whether the turbine generator is going to work.

Selling into a buying circle is hard work. Marketers must craft messages that are maximally relevant to the needs and interests of each party. It's a creative challenge, requiring considerable research and data collection.

To plan your campaigns effectively, know the players and their roles:

- **Specifier.** Technical expert, engineer, or IT specialist who develops the specifications for the features and functions needed.

- **Influencer.** Someone who benefits directly and significantly from the purchase. Can be, but is not necessarily, also a user of the product. For example, a professional in a law firm who needs to buy 500 laptops has strong opinions for the features of the laptop the firm provides.

- **User.** Someone who uses the product regularly to get the job done.

- **Decision-maker.** Department head or senior person with final sign-off authority.

- **Gatekeeper.** Someone who stands between the seller and any of the participants—for instance, an administrative assistant or mailroom employee.

- **Buyer.** The purchasing agent who actually places the order.

- **Buying committee, also known as buying circle.** A group assembled for the purpose of managing this purchase. The committee can comprise of the previous people and others.

It's important to know the players' motivations, as illustrated in Table 2.1. Senior managers will likely want higher level productivity gains. Users want a product that's easy to learn and operate. The purchasing agent might be motivated by credit terms and the like. Specifiers need a level of technical information that might make someone else's eyes glaze over. Keep in mind that individuals can play more than one role in the process; for example, a gatekeeper can also be an influencer.

Table 2.1   Motivating Various Members of the Buying Committee

Buying Role	Motivations
Specifier	Asks how this thing is different from its competitors
Influencer	Wants to be sure the product makes his/her job easier
User	Concerned with whether the product is easy to install and use
Decision-maker	Focused on the bottom-line results
Gatekeeper	Has the mission of protecting the boss from sales people
Purchasing agent	Rewarded for saving money and buying efficiently

May I Have This Dance?

Buyers without sellers, and vice versa, are like dancers without partners, each spinning around the ballroom alone. They might pair up or they might not. It depends on what happens during the first simple steps, which are:

1. The buyer identifies a problem. For example, the company's copiers are too old to meet today's standards for speed, convenience, and quality.

2. The buyer identifies a solution. For example, let's buy some new copiers.

3. The seller (you) has the solution to the buyer's problem. We sell copiers with all the latest bells and whistles.

But you have a problem of your own, which is how do you make the buyer aware that you can solve his problem? Your campaign strategy—to get noticed—is the important next step.

Make sure the buyer knows you exist. Advertise in trade publications and on search engines, and spend on PR. Get some buzz going about your product so that when the buyer moves to the next step—researching a number of vendors—you make the list. At that point, you need a new strategy: showing how you stand out from the competition. For this, you might consider speaking at conventions and creating useful collateral material.

After the dance has begun, you can control—or at least influence—the choreography. The important thing is to stimulate the buyer to make a first move: to express the desire to dance. Every business marketer has some variation in his go-to-market process, perhaps involving resellers and distributors, or using a hybrid model wherein the most efficient sales resource is assigned to each stage of the selling process. But the fundamental process is the same, and marketers who analyze the process and break it down can figure out how to turn it to their advantage. They will know exactly when and how to generate leads for their sales team.

Table 2.2 maps the selling process to the buying process. Follow the buying process from top to bottom, noticing that it follows a logical flow. Notice also that at each step, the seller's processes and objectives change accordingly. The types of campaigns that are most effective will change too, encompassing everything from PR to face-to-face sales and support.

Table 2.2   Typical Buying Process and Selling Process

Buying Process	Selling Process	Seller's Objective	Campaign Types
Identify need.	Arouse interest.	Arouse interest.	Advertise and do PR.
Research solutions.	Identify a company with a need.	Be known to research team.	Advertise, use PR, and use social media (SEM, SEO, and blogs).
Develop short list.	Create preference.	Be selected for the short list.	Use direct mail, email, telephone, website, and collateral.
Request proposals and quotes.	Propose specifically.	Submit a winning proposal.	Use face-to-face sales and inside sales.
Review proposals and quotes.	Attempt to influence.	Create preference.	Use face-to-face sales, direct mail, webinars, road shows, blogs, and podcasts.
Negotiate.	Negotiate.	Preserve margins.	Use face-to-face sales and inside sales.
Select a vendor.	Compare to competition.	Win.	Use face-to-face sales.
Install and use.	Enhance usage.	Satisfaction and usage.	Use support personnel, a website, e-newsletters, user groups, and social media.
Upgrade.	Identify need.	Up sell and cross sell.	Use telesales, direct mail, client conferences, social media, and webinars.

How Will You Know When You're There?

Setting clear objectives is your first step in campaign planning. Without them, you won't be able to measure success or failure.

Typically, marketers set objectives such as:

- The number of leads expected
- The degree of required qualification for each lead
- When the leads will arrive
- The cost per lead
- Lead-to-sales conversion ratio
- The potential revenue per lead
- Campaign return on investment (ROI) or expense-to-revenue ratio

You can refine objectives by sales territory, industry, or market segment; leads into new accounts; new contacts within an existing account (penetration); or leads into competitive accounts. But the most important thing is the plan. Don't spend a penny until you have a realistic plan to generate the right number of qualified leads needed by your sales organization.

With all the planning of the front end, don't leave the back end unattended. Plan your fulfillment materials and make sure the necessary people are standing by to capture, fulfill, qualify, and nurture the flow of leads you generate.

The Goldilocks School of Lead Flow Planning

When it comes to leads, it's tempting to think that more is better. But the truth is, enough is—well, enough. You don't want so few leads that the sales territories cannot comfortably fulfill their quotas, but you don't want so many that they cannot all be serviced. You want a number of leads that is just right.

Calculating Conversations

How do you arrive at that magic number? One way is to go to the source: the sales managers and reps. Ask them what their lead requirements are. Become informed by reading the sales plan. Learn how your company's compensation plan works so you can understand their business and personal objectives. All this input is crucial to mapping your campaign strategies.

Through these conversations, you're likely to find that each rep wants a certain number of qualified leads per day, week, or month. The reps may make specific requests by product category, industry, sales territory, or whatever else is defining their quotas. Gather as many of these details as you can. Each one will help make this campaign a success for you and for them.

Just keep in mind that sales reps want what they want—and they can be unrealistic. If they say, "Give me everything," or "Give me only leads that are ready to close this month," try this next method.

Do-It-Yourself

Another way is to do some quick calculations yourself. Use the reps' sales quotas to back your way into the number of leads required by determining their sales productivity per lead. This approach gives you some validation in future conversations and is useful when dealing with reps who want the moon.

You need three numbers from sales and finance:

- The average revenue quota per rep.

- The average revenue per order.

- The percent of revenue that the sales people generate naturally, *without* the help of leads, repeat sales, or deeper penetration within the account, as well as referrals. (You may have to ask around sales management and reps to come up with this figure.)

The sample worksheet in Table 2.3 shows the process using some hypothetical numbers. As you can see in this example, reps need 150 qualified leads to make their quota. (Note for all tables: / = divided by; * = multiplied by.)

Table 2.3   Lead Requirements Worksheet

Process	Calculations
Revenue quota per rep	$3,000,000
Percent of quota self-generated	40%
Quota requiring lead support ($3M * 1 − .40)	$1,800,000
Revenue per order	$60,000
Converting leads required ($1.8M / $60K)	30 leads
Conversion rate	20%
Qualified leads required per rep (30 / .20)	150 leads

 Tip

Don't be surprised if salespeople ask you to pass along every inquiry that pertains to their territories and accounts. Don't be surprised—but don't do it. Reps are likely to cherry-pick leads, tossing out the ones they don't like and wasting your marketing investment. If you pass unqualified leads, they'll lose sight of the value of the lead-generation program and leave potential customers hanging—or on their way to the nearest competitor.

A Few Last Words on Lead Flow Planning

As you plan your lead flow, keep in mind the following:

- **A steady pace wins the race.** Don't flood your sales teams, but don't make them suffer through droughts either. Aim for a steady stream of leads by month. Analyze past campaign results to note peaks and valleys, and schedule actions with short planning horizons, such as a direct response print ad, banner ads, or outbound telemarketing or email to smooth things out.

Show the same consideration for the resources in the middle of the process—your response handlers and qualifiers. An overload does not just strain them, but it can annoy customers.

- **Plan for the unexpected.** Don't be forced to scramble at the last minute when something out of the ordinary, such as a new product introduction or an end-of-fiscal sales push, suddenly occurs. In most companies, these special events happen with some frequency. Check with product management so you can plan lead requirements ahead.

- **Know when to play hard and fast.** Hard offers, such as "have a sales rep call me," convert faster. Use them when you need a quick fix at the end of fiscal periods or can't spare the staff or financial resources to nurture a prospect pool.

- **Open up the circle.** Include everyone in your planning process—sales people, call center or outsourced service, marketing department, and finance—so they'll all feel a sense of ownership of the campaign. Be prepared to communicate often, explaining activities and restating benefits.

CALCULATING CAMPAIGN VOLUME REQUIREMENTS

How much campaigning is required to generate a month of leads for a sales team? Use this simple process to determine a predictable, manageable, and timely lead flow.

1. Estimate the number of qualified leads each sales rep can reasonably be expected to follow up on a month.

2. Multiply that number by the number of reps in a geographic territory.

3. Then divide by the qualification rate you expect for your campaign inquiries.

4. Divide again by the expected response rate on the campaign. This final number is the campaign volume needed to support that territory for a month. In mail campaigns, you can control the lead flow in the territory by selecting ZIP codes for each volume required. In other media,

you might end up with some peaks and valleys that you can smooth out with tactical campaign efforts such as telemarketing and email.

5. Continue the process for each territory, and add up the results. You will have total numbers for your qualified leads, inquiries, and campaign volumes for the month.

Planning for Your Campaign Budget

Campaign budgeting can be extremely complicated in lead generation because there are so many moving parts. You need not only the usual costs of creating and executing the campaign. You also need to account for fulfillment expense, qualification expense, and lead-management expense. Costs need to be gathered from your call centers, your support staffs, and your vendors. The best approach is to involve your finance people in helping you with some of the cost accounting that is necessary to create accurate view of what things cost on a fixed and variable basis.

That said, you can also approach budgeting from a top-down perspective, and keep things fairly simple. The main objective of budgeting is to be sure you are delivering a positive ROI, one that meets the expectations your company sets for marketing investments. Let's look at a couple of straightforward approaches that can help you.

But first, consider the following argument: In business marketing, sales people usually are responsible for sales quotas in the millions of dollars—certainly in the hundreds of thousands per year. Their salaries and benefit packages might begin in the low six figures. So give a thought to the expense—and the opportunity cost—of a sales person working on cold prospecting, or on underdeveloped, unqualified leads. You might argue that marketing cannot possibly spend enough to offset the expense of unproductive sales efforts. Taking this argument to its logical conclusion, any investment in lead generation and qualification appears to be money worth spending.

But of course you want to do the right thing. You not only want each lead to be productive, but you also want to prove that each lead pays for itself. So let us turn now to some calculations.

Calculating an Allowable Cost Per Lead

One of the most important budgeting factors in lead generation is making sure you deliver leads to sales at an affordable price. To calculate the allowable cost per lead, begin with the total direct campaign costs, including all fixed and variable costs that can be directly attributed to the campaign. This includes creative and pre-production work, cost of developing and producing fulfillment materials, and the normal variable costs of campaign development and execution. Divide this amount by the number of expected campaign responses to get your cost per inquiry.

Next, you need an estimate for the costs associated with qualifying a lead. If you try to determine this number on a per campaign basis, you will quickly be forced to run screaming from the room. The sane alternative is to calculate an average qualification cost for inquiries over a set period, such as a year. So gather up all the back-end inquiry-handling costs, the direct headcount involved in inquiry capture, fulfillment, qualification, and nurturing. (If your back-end processes are out-sourced, gathering the data is as simple as adding up the bills.) After you have a number for the year, divide it by the number of inquiries handled in the year. This number will serve as your average cost to qualify an inquiry.

The next step is to gather data from finance and sales. You need the average order size, namely, the total revenue divided by the total number of orders. (This number appeared in Table 2.3 as a hypothetical $60,000.) You need the margin (or its opposite, the cost of goods sold) and the direct sales expense per order, calculated by the total sales expense divided by the total number of orders.

Now let's look at an example of how this works. Table 2.4 works through some hypothetical numbers to arrive at a cost of lead closed and an allowable cost per lead, and compares the two. Your objective is that the cost of a closed lead is lower than the allowable. If it's higher, you lose money on the campaign.

Table 2.4 Calculating Your Campaign's Allowable Cost Per Lead

Cost per inquiry (campaign cost / number of responses)	$100
Average cost to qualify an inquiry (back-end handling costs / inquiries per year)	$50
Total cost per inquiry qualified (cost per inquiry + cost to qualify)	$150
Lead qualification rate	25%
Cost of qualified lead (cost per lead / qualification rate)	$600
Lead conversion rate	30%
Cost of a closed lead (cost of qualified lead / conversion rate)	**$2,000**
Average order size (annual revenue / number of orders)	$10,000
Net margin per order (revenue per order * margin, 60%)	$6,000
Allowable cost per lead (net margin per order – direct sales expense, $3,500)	**$2,500**

To get to allowable cost per lead, it's not actually necessary to know how many inquiries will be generated, qualified, and converted. Instead, you need to know the cost per inquiry, the cost to qualify an inquiry, the qualification and conversion rates, the net margin per order, and the direct sales expense per order.

In this hypothetical example, say the campaign spent $15,000 and generated 150 inquiries. Whatever the cost and the responses, the important number is the cost per inquiry. Here, we have hypothesized it as $100. Separately, the average cost to qualify an inquiry for the year was calculated at $50. We divide the qualification rate (25 percent) into the total cost per inquiry qualified ($150) to calculate the cost of a qualified lead. Then, we divide that by the conversion rate (30 percent) to get the cost of a closed lead ($2,000). This number is then compared with the allowable cost per closed lead ($2,500), which is a simple calculation of the net margin per order minus the cost of sales (hypothetically set here as $3,500). In this example, the campaign looks promising, because the expected cost per converted lead is $500 less than the allowable cost per lead.

If you put this information in a spreadsheet and play with it, you can quickly see how much leverage there is on the back-end, meaning after the lead has come in and you are working it through qualification and nurturing. A few efficiencies on qualification rate and conversion rate work wonders on campaign ROI.

Establishing Break-Even Campaign Response Rates

Another useful approach to campaign budgeting is figuring out what kind of response rate is needed to break even on your outbound campaign. With the break-even number in hand, you can eyeball the pro forma numbers and decide whether you feel comfortable with the likelihood of making that response rate when the campaign is run. If you decide you need more wiggle room, then you need to adjust your numbers to suit, whether by lowering variable costs or improving the power of the offer, or whatever gets you the pro forma numbers that you think your campaign can deliver.

Calculating the break-even begins with the same calculation we just performed, to identify the allowable cost per lead closed. It then works back from the allowable cost per closed lead, to the allowable cost per lead qualified, to the allowable cost per inquiry, and ultimately to the response rate required to break even.

Working with the same hypothetical numbers, Table 2.5 shows what this might look like.

Table 2.5   Calculating Break-Even Campaign Response Rates

Average order size (annual revenue / number of orders)	$10,000
Net margin per order (revenue per order * margin, 60%)	$6,000
Allowable cost per closed lead (net margin per order – direct sales expense, $3,500)	**$2,500**
Lead conversion rate	30%
Allowable cost per qualified lead (allowable cost per lead * conversion rate)	$750
Inquiry qualification rate	25%
Allowable cost per inquiry (allowable cost per qualified lead * qualification rate)	$187.50
Campaign cost per piece (at $1500 CPM)	$1.50
Break-even campaign response rate (cost per piece / allowable cost per inquiry	.8%

In this case, you ask yourself whether you can be fairly sure you'll get at least .8 percent, or 8 responses per 1,000. If that doesn't feel realistic, you need to lower your CPM, strengthen your offers and media, or improve your qualification or conversion rates.

3

The Marketing Database: Not Sexy, But Essential to Success

Data drives lead generation. Seems like a no-brainer, right? After all, without information about customers and prospects, how can leads be generated? But of equal importance to the data is a system that allows it to be collected, maintained, accessed and analyzed so it can be used to select the appropriate targets for marketing communications and sales activities—the core activities of lead generation. Enter the marketing database.

The marketing database (MDB) is critical for any marketer, but it is arguably even more important for business marketers than for consumer organizations because of the high value of each account. A business marketing database is also much more complex than its consumer cousin, for several reasons:

- In consumer purchasing, the decision-maker and the buyer are usually the same person—a one-man show. In business buying, there's an entire cast of characters. In the mix are employees charged with product specifications, users of the product, and purchasing agents. A properly constructed MDB stores the intelligence that enables marketers to identify these buying roles, and differentiate customer treatment accordingly.

- In addition to capturing standard information, business marketing databases must aggregate information from specific business addresses, known as *sites* or *locations*, with the umbrella company or enterprise to which they belong.

Data Sources and Types

There are numerous ways to classify data, but these three approaches are particularly helpful to business marketers:

1. Behavioral data versus descriptive data
2. Customer data versus prospect data
3. Internal data versus external data

The following sections describe each category.

Behavioral Versus Descriptive Data

Behavioral data ("what they do") refers to elements that record a customer's actions, such as purchase, inquiry, response to a campaign, payment, complaint, website visit, customer service call, and so on. Past behavior being a strong predictor of future behavior, behavioral data is generally more valuable than descriptive for analytical and campaign selection purposes.

Descriptive data ("what they look like") refers to elements that describe the customer's appearance. These might be elements such as company size, industry, geographic location, and other "firmographic" fields such as number of years in business.

Customer Versus Prospect Data

Customer data is information about current and former customers as well as other contacts who have not yet purchased anything but have shown some sort of interest in your company. These are known as *inquirers* and can be campaign respondents, visitors to your booth at a trade show or people who have registered at your website. Technically, these people are prospects, but they're more qualified than cold prospects, and they are worth nurturing along, in the expectation that they can be converted to buyers. Data about customers and inquirers comprises the heart of any business-to-business (B-to-B) marketing database.

Prospect data is the customer and inquirer data that is usually maintained in the MDB, but data about non-inquirer prospects is most often rented or licensed as needed. One reason for this practice is that maintaining data is expensive and time-consuming. Another is that because prospect data tends to be readily available, it's usually more efficient to acquire it for a particular campaign or analytic project. Yet another reason is that fresher names are more likely to respond than stale ones, so marketers prefer to acquire fresh names at the last possible moment, rather than keeping them on hand.

That being said, many B-to-B marketers do maintain prospect data in certain situations:

- When the target audience is small and multiple touches are needed to drive the response, it often pays to purchase prospect data for ongoing use.

- When the prospect list is cheaper or easier to license and hold than it is to rent for one-time use.

Internal Data Versus External Data

Internal Data

Internal data ("the meat and potatoes of your MDB") captured through sales contact files, billing systems, operating systems, customer service systems, and your company's website provides the core of your marketing database. Most of the data pertains to current and former customers and inquirers. Here's a look at some typical internal data sources, with pros, cons, and caveats.

Sales Contact Files

Field sales and inside sales teams are likely to have the best information about customers and prospects because they are in regular touch with their sales targets. The quality and accessibility of a sales force's files generally varies according to the size of the company. Large companies with big sales forces may have a customized, sophisticated sales force automation (SFA) system like Microsoft Dynamics CRM or Salesforce.com. SFA tools are typically designed for easy data transfer, in and out. Smaller companies often use off-the-shelf tools, even spreadsheets, and these can be supplemented with interfaces to enable data to port easily.

However, before you can transfer the data, you need to have it in hand, and that can be a challenge. In B-to-B, where a sales team is the primary "owner" of the customer relationship, the SFA tool is of paramount importance to sales force productivity and thus to revenue generation. Salespeople can be ferociously protective of their contact information. Here are a few ways to get their buy-in:

- At the very least, you need to initiate plenty of communication about how lead generation will benefit them and the company as a whole.

- You might have to go a bit further, like offering something of obvious value such as a proprietary newsletter or white paper that they won't want their accounts to miss.

- Or think about this: A little inclusion can go a long way. Offer to make salespeople part of the marketing messages to their customers by using their names as signatory on direct mail letters or email correspondence.

There is a caveat. The best use of SFA is as a feeder to a robust MDB, versus a marketing database in itself. If you try to run your lead generation campaigns using only a sales force automation system as your database, you will find it wanting. SFA tools are a rich source of data, but they are not designed to:

- Support the kinds of queries marketers need to ask to gain insights and plan campaigns.

- Hold the kinds of information—purchase history and promotional history, for example—that marketers need for analysis.

- Also, data standards on accuracy and completeness are impossible to maintain in SFA systems because many users are allowed to enter data. That said, your company's SFA might be a reasonable interim tool, until you have enough volume and urgency to move to a fully functional MDB.

 Tip

Just because a contact name is available from an internal source does not mean that it is useful for marketing purposes. You should examine these contacts before adding them into your MDB and arrange for regular updates to keep the data current.

Accounting Systems

Many small businesses keep their customer lists on accounting systems such as Quickbooks. These systems enable a certain amount of data accessibility and sortability and can offer important customer purchase history. They also supply credit worthiness data, revealing how, when and if customers pay—data that gives valuable insight to account preferences and credit worthiness. The accounting system in your company—large or small—will be an important feeder of useful customer information to your MDB.

There is a caveat. The contact-level data from billing systems is likely to be from a person in an administrative function, not a decision-maker. If you associate this contact with large order values, you might be knocking on the wrong door.

Operating and Fulfillment Systems

An operating database is designed to run business operations like accounting, inventory, shipping, payroll, and supply chain management. Examples include enterprise resources planning tool (ERP) and e-commerce tools.

Operations data can yield valuable information about a customer's preferences—for instance, whether a customer is most comfortable communicating by mail, phone, or in person through a visit from a field representative or distributor. This data can be used to predict behavior and indicate the best channels to reach customers.

Operating systems also supply frequency data, which can give insights into customers' purchase patterns, and shipping preference, which might be useful. For example, a customer who consistently requests overnight delivery is a costly account to serve.

There is a caveat. Don't plan to use operating systems data to analyze long-term customer behavioral history. These systems tend to send older data into an archive, so you have to take special steps to pull earlier data for analytic purposes.

Customer Service Systems

Customer service contacts are generally complaints, and who wants complaint files in a marketing database? You do, for two reasons:

- A customer whose complaint has been resolved is likely to turn into a loyal buyer.

- Complaints are generally assigned a code by type of complaint, and these codes might give insights about the customer and your company's relationship with the account.

There is a caveat. Some customer service systems enable comments, which do not translate into selectable data, meaning data that can be classified and accessed for analytic purposes. Comments are meant to be read. Data in an MDB is meant to be selected, counted, compared, analyzed, and exported. In short, open-ended comments do not belong in a marketing database.

Inquiry Files

Inquirers have shown interest by asking for more information or requesting further contact. Inquiry files are fed by outbound campaigns, print advertising, trade shows, and seminars or Internet-sourced contacts and can be a valuable addition to your marketing database.

Website Data

Your company's website is a rich environment for generating names of customers and prospects. It's a good idea to include a registration request at your website, with a motivational offer like a white paper or case study download, to convert anonymous visitors into contacts with whom you can maintain an ongoing relationship. If you are conducting e-commerce, your web data will be an even more important source of information for your marketing database.

External Data

External data is for "filling in the blanks." After your database has a solid foundation of internal data, you can round it out with data from external sources. An important source of external data is lists of prospects, whether compiled lists or response lists. Another way to expand your database is through data append, whereby your records are compared to a large external database, and you select for purchase the particular extra data elements that you don't have in house. Many marketers find they need to supplement the usual external data sources with additional data gathered by hand, in a process known as data discovery. And last, the potential of social networks to supply lead-generation data is a surface barely scratched and possibly miles deep.

Prospect Lists

One reason direct mail continues to be a powerful medium for lead generation is the abundant supply of lists available for rent. Lists of businesses usable for prospecting are typically rented through specialized brokers, such as Merit Direct, or the business-to-business divisions of Direct Media and American List Counsel (ALC). More than 40,000 business lists are available for rent, at prices ranging from $50 per thousand (M) to more than $200/M. See Table 3.1 for details on the range of lists available and Table 3.2 for current pricing by list type.

Table 3.1   Postal List Availability in the United States

List Category	Quantities
B-to-B postal mail lists	40,290
Lists offering telephone numbers	20,384
Lists offering email addresses	12,074
Mainstream postal lists (regular usage by mailers)	1,600
Very actively used postal lists	350

Source: David Gaudreau, Direct Media

Table 3.2   Business List Prices

List Category	Average Price per Thousand
Business magazines, controlled circulation	$145
Business magazines, paid circulation	$135
Business merchandise buyers	$116
Permission-based email B-to-B	$285

Source: Worldata, Winter 2009 Price Index

Business lists often focus more on the job title or function than the individual person, and they come in two general types, compiled files and response files:

- **Compiled lists.** Compiled lists are created from directories or other public and private sources for the purpose of resale or rental to marketers. The names have some characteristic in common, whether it's geographic or demographic, or related to industry, job function or product type. Dun & Bradstreet and InfoUSA are the two largest compilers of original business data. The compiled data might be sorted, repackaged, and sold by other companies, like Experian and Acxiom, or by list brokers and managers.

  Compiled files are usually fairly inexpensive, around $50/M to $100/M. They generally offer good generic selectable variables, like Standard Industrial Classification code (SIC), phone number, and details about the company's location and its relation to a corporate entity. Suitable prospects for just about any business category are available, such as federal government buyers, schoolteachers, professionals in technology, law, real estate and healthcare—you name the group, there's probably a list. See Table 3.3 for a few examples.

Table 3.3 Examples of Industry-Specific Compiled Lists

Target Audience	Compiled List
Government buyers	Federal Direct
Schools	MDR
Installed technology at companies	Harte-Hanks Ci Technology Database
Insurance	A.M. Best
Pension and benefits managers	Judy Diamond Associates
Hospitals and institutions	MCH
Marketing professionals	The List, Inc.

 Tip

If you can't get the names of particular individual prospects at companies that are in your target audience, you can prospect effectively using just the job function, known as *title slug* in direct mail, without an actual person's name. Because people change jobs so often, you might find it more productive to reach target audiences by mailing this way.

There is a caveat. Compiled lists vary in coverage, accuracy, and completeness. It is worthwhile to sample lists from more than one compiler to find out which produces the best results in your target market. It is also advisable to test lists on small samples before making a full-scale commitment to importing data from a compiler.

 Tip

Dun & Bradstreet (D&B) data was originally compiled to assess company credit worthiness, so D&B data for medium- and large-sized firms tends to be most complete. InfoGroup data first was originally compiled from Yellow Pages phone directories, so it tends to offer broad market coverage, even among small firms, but might provide less richness about any given company.

- **Response lists.** Response lists are created as a by-product of other businesses, like catalog sales, seminars, trade organization memberships, or magazine and newsletter subscriptions. A sampling of lists and list categories appears in Table 3.4. These lists tend to be more accurate than compiled lists, and they usually contain some information about product interest or buying authority. The fact that the names have joined, subscribed, or otherwise taken a business action indicates that they are "responsive," and might be better prospects for lead generation than a name plucked out of a directory.

Selects available with response lists are similar to those in the consumer world, for example, subscription recency and acquisition source. But publication files often are able to offer other selects as well, such as title, function, company size, buying authority, and products purchased.

Not surprisingly, response lists are priced higher than compiled files, ranging from $95/M to $150/M. Some files, such as high-tech industry lists, run as high as $175/M to $250/M range.

There is a caveat. Response files represent a self-selected group, and thus cannot be construed as complete universes of all the potential prospects in a category. Also, they are less likely to have additional data available for targeted selection.

Table 3.4   Major B-to-B Response List Categories

Categories	Examples
Office supplies	Viking Office Products, Staples, and OfficeMax
Seminar and training companies	Fred Pryor, American Management Association, National Seminars, and Skillpath
General business publishing	Business Week and McGraw-Hill
Technology publishing	CMP, Ziff-Davis, IDG, and Tech Target
Newsletters	Clement Communications, Briefing Publishing, Aspen Publishers, and Harvard Business School Publishing
Back office supplies	C & H Distributors, Harbor Freight, Chiswick, and National Business Furniture
Food and gift	B-to-B files of Omaha Steaks, Mrs. Beasley's Cakes, and LL Bean
Industrial products and trade publications	New Pig, Seton Name Plate, Advanced Packaging, and Adhesives Age
Compiled information	D&B, InfoUSA, Harte-Hanks Market Intelligence, and idEXEC

Source: David Gaudreau, Direct Media

Prospecting Databases

Recently, some large mailers ("large" meaning mail volumes of over 10 million pieces annually) have started to develop proprietary prospecting databases as a way to lower costs and increase the list options available to them. Typically, these private databases are built and maintained by the list broker or manager, assembled from rental lists that have proven the most productive for the company. Proprietary databases have a lot to offer, namely fast and convenient access to pre-deduplicated names that have appropriate appends in place, with approvals already secured.

But you don't have to mail a million to reap the benefits of prospecting databases. Companies large and small can access commercially available prospecting databases, which come in two types—both offering a gigantic number of prospects:

- **Member databases (to take names out, you must put your own in).** Examples: Abacus B2B Alliance (122 million names) and B2bBase, a joint venture of MeritDirect and Experian (8 million multi-buyers).

- **Open cooperative databases, de-duplicated from multiple lists, where you pay only for what you use.** Examples: MeritDirect's MeritBase (60 million names), Direct Media's b2bdatawarehouse (100 million names), and Mardev DM2's Decisionmaker Database (50 million names).

Email Lists

Two facts about email lists will probably come as no surprise: They are increasingly available; and anti-spam technology, among other factors, has significantly impacted their prospecting productivity. Although email is still an effective tool for current customer marketing such as lead nurturing, up-sell, cross-sell, and retention, many business marketers are reporting lower cost per lead results using direct mail versus email for cold prospects, because buyers tend not to open email from unknown sources.

Pricing for email lists is changing quickly, because the industry is so new. Prices now range from $200/M to around $300/M. Many list owners currently add another $100/M for delivery, but there is pressure to make this practice disappear. Meanwhile, you should feel free to negotiate prices aggressively.

There is a caveat. Email is more susceptible to data decay than other marketing channels. Almost one-third of business email addresses change annually.

Appended Information

Business marketers can enhance their customer information by appending to their house file certain data elements purchased from third-party data vendors, who have in turn acquired rights to them from owners of large compiled business databases. You can overlay your file with such important data fields as industrial classification code, title, phone number, credit rating, executive contacts and company size at a low cost, ranging from 15 cents to $6 per piece matched, depending on the data element required. Compared to collecting the data directly from customers and prospects, data append is a fast and convenient way to enrich your database, for purposes of research, analysis, modeling, and lead generation campaign selection.

As a process, data append in B-to-B is no different from that performed on consumer files. Before you begin, you must decide on the fields you want to append. Although appended data is cheaper than proactively collected data, there is still a cost associated with it. So only buy the data elements that will drive measurable value for your lead generation program.

Keep in mind that matching B-to-B files is far more difficult than consumer files. B-to-B files can have a company name, a title, or an individual name on line one. So, although this inconsistency causes no problem with postal delivery, it does mean that computerized matching of the company name on your file to the company name on the append file requires sophisticated software.

 Tip

Businesses can take advantage of several services that append email addresses to their house files. Some services investigate the email address conventions at major companies, and then impute the likely email address of employees. Another approach is creating large databases of email addresses and postal addresses, and conducting a match against your house file.

Data Discovery

Most business marketers are focused on a relatively narrow target audience—optical engineers, for example, or accountants. When your entire universe of prospects is limited, you want to be sure you have access to every possible company or contact in the target. Furthermore, you might want to ensure that your database is populated with specific, important data elements about each account.

This kind of breadth and depth is rarely available from commercial data sources. So many B-to-B marketers rely on a discovery process, whereby they call into key target accounts and gather the needed data by hand. This process is sometimes called *contact discovery* or *list building*.

The first rule of contact discovery is: Don't do it until you have exhausted other, less expensive routes, like data append. Expect to pay $7 to $25 per discovered contact, depending on the qualifications you want. The second rule is: Use a reputable call center with experience in B-to-B data discovery.

THE THREE STAGES OF DATA DISCOVERY

Data discovery best follows a three-stage process, as recommended by Dennis Totah, the founder of Catapult Target Profiling and a pioneer in the field of contact discovery:

1. Buy first. Get what you can from third parties, before investing in any work to generate data on your own.

2. Identify the holes, and verify or validate the data in your database. This can be done relatively cheaply through Internet searches and web-based tools like LinkedIn and Jigsaw. Or you might choose to verify using the more expensive method of outbound calling. A key advantage of phoning is that you not only find out whether a contact is still at the firm, you also can capture the name of the replacement executive in the case where the person has left the job.

3. Build, adding contact names, titles, and other key data elements, using outbound telephone calls.

New Internet-Based Data Sources

As social media takes the marketing world by storm, one of its most valuable applications in B-to-B marketing is in the area of data compilation. Several new websites are creating entirely new data sources:

- **Jigsaw.** Jigsaw users upload contact information—as of this writing, more than 26 million contacts, and growing by 20,000 new records daily—including company name, contact name, site address, phone, fax, and email. Jigsaw then confirms that the listing represents a real business with a ping to the company website. For uploading information, users earn points that they can spend to download new contacts and create prospect lists. They lose points if other users spot incorrect information—creating automatic data cleansing.

  So you get clean data and wait, there's more: When you download data from Jigsaw, you own it and you can use it as many times as you want. Jigsaw also offers a nifty data cleansing service to help you update the contacts on your house file.

- **ZoomInfo.** ZoomInfo performs automated scanning of the Internet for business information and merge-purges it into a gigantic list of companies and contacts, available to marketers and sales people.

  ZoomInfo lets you not only search names based on criteria typical in B-to-B, like company size, industry, and title or job function, but also lets you select targets based on the information gleaned from press releases, such as whether someone has joined a new company or left an old one. According to ZoomInfo officials, the system updates 30 million profiles a day, with users voluntarily updating another 10,000 of their own profiles weekly.

- **LinkedIn.** Pioneering social site LinkedIn is an exceptionally good tool for finding people in target companies and networking your way to introductions. As a data resource for marketing campaigns, LinkedIn is not even in the running. It doesn't own the data, and thus can't make it available in bulk to marketers.

   However, B-to-B direct marketers are looking for creative ways to take advantage of the LinkedIn database. OneSource, a high-end global business data supplier owned by InfoGROUP, offers a widget to its Global Business Browser that enables clients who are looking at a particular target company on the OneSource database to instantly view the company employees that are already in that client's LinkedIn network. "With LinkedIn's three degrees of separation, a small number of contacts can represent a million-name network," says Sham R. Sao, CMO of OneSource. "OneSource users now have the option of approaching their targets through personal LinkedIn introductions instead of cold calling."

- **Demandbase.** Most B-to-B marketers have traditionally sourced campaign data through brokers, or, when using online data sources, through subscription-based services like SalesGenie and Hoover's. But for a Web 2.0 world, where user expectations for ease of use and flexibility in e-commerce are at an all-time high, Demandbase has created a concept that is changing how business marketers can access prospecting data.

   Like many compilers, Demandbase aggregates business data from multiple sources, among them D&B, Hoovers, LexisNexis, and ZoomInfo. They then extract the "best" element from each source, using a proprietary algorithm that compares duplicates and identifies which one to keep.

   Demandbase's process feels like retail, with a shopping cart and the kinds of functionality you find at Amazon or Apple. More important, the contents of your cart are priced by the item. So marketers with narrowly targeted campaigns—which happens all the time in B-to-B—can order up as few or as many names as needed. "We think we're selling to a 'business consumer,'" says Chris Golec, founder and CEO. "Many business marketers simply can't use 5,000-name minimum orders."

Data Fields You Need for Lead Generation

The data fields shown in Table 3.5 are those typically maintained by business marketers. Each industry and each company adjusts this list as applicable to their specific needs.

Table 3.5   Data Fields Used in Business Marketing Databases

Data Elements	Considerations
Company name, address, company general phone, fax, website	The company name at a particular site, or postal address, plus site-level information, like general phone number, fax, and website.
Contact name (s), direct phone, direct fax, mobile phone, email, Twitter handle, LinkedIn URL, blog URL	Multiple individuals (known as *contacts*) and their contact information, in all relevant forms. In this field, you use the contact's direct phone number, if available.
Contact title, function, buying role	You want to collect both an official title plus a true job function for each contact because titles can be somewhat obscure and meaningless these days. Thus, it is a good idea to identify the job functions that are important to your selling process, and attach a predefined, standardized function to each contact. Also useful is an indicator of the contact's role in the buying process, such as decision-maker, specifier, or influencer.
Enterprise link	Some sites represent stand-alone companies, but often company sites are a part of a larger enterprise, including a headquarters and multiple business addresses. Be sure to connect sites to whatever "parent" firm is involved.
SIC or NAICS industrial classification code	The U.S. government is currently in the process of migrating the four-digit Standard Industrial Classification (SIC) system, a leftover from the 1930s, to a new six-digit system, North American Industry Classification System (NAICS), which was officially launched in 1997. NAICS was developed in cooperation with Canada and Mexico. (You can read about it in depth at www.census.gov/epcd/www/naics.html.) NAICS is a more modern classification system, reflecting the new realities of how our information economy operates. The migration process is a difficult one, so progress is slow, albeit steady. Search for SIC codes by keyword, and vice versa, at www.osha.gov/oshstats/sicser.html. Note: Some companies use their own internally defined industry indicator as a supplement to or replacement of SIC.

Table 3.5   Data Fields Used in Business Marketing Databases (continued)

Data Elements	Considerations
Year started in business	As is logical, an older firm is more likely to demonstrate stable buying patterns than a newer one.
Public versus private	Another indicator of buying behavior.
Revenue or sales	It is relatively easy to find revenue levels for publicly traded firms. Capture revenue at the site level or the enterprise level according to which is more meaningful for your business.
Employee size	At public companies, employee size might be a useful additional data element for predicting marketing opportunity. For privately held companies, where revenue figures are not available, the number of employees can be a powerful alternate indicator of purchase propensity and buying process.
Purchase history	Capturing what the account has purchased in the past, the date, the amount, the order placement method, the payment method, and the frequency, provides information that is highly predictive of future purchase propensity. Ideally, you want to keep track of each outbound touch and link it to the purchase, for a closed-loop picture. Maintaining return information adds to the veracity of the purchase history.
Credit score	Use either an internally generated indicator or a commercially available score from a provider like Dun & Bradstreet or Experian.
Yellow Pages advertising	As old-fashioned as it might seem, in some industries the extent to which the company actively promotes itself in the Yellow Pages can be a predictive variable. Even better, this information is often available. Originally, much B-to-B data was compiled from phone book records, and the ad size was listed as part of the Yellow Pages publisher's company record. Marketers later found it to have some predictive value, so data compilers continue to make it available.
Product history	The history should include the price, category, SKU numbers, and product names of items purchased. If the purchased product was later removed or uninstalled, keep a record of that, too.
Budget, purchase plans	In some industries, this data might be published by research or analyst firms and made available to marketers.

continued

Table 3.5   Data Fields Used in Business Marketing Databases (continued)

Data Elements	Considerations
Purchase preferences, such as channel	Details about how the account likes to buy—its preferred channel, terms, and other information—might be predictive. By all means, maintain customer preference relating to opting out of receiving communications from you through various channels, particularly email and telephone.
Answers to qualification questions	If your company has developed standard qualification questions around such sales-readiness indicators as budget, authority, need, and timeframe, and if your company has a scoring system in place, this data is helpful for sorting and selecting campaign targets.
Answers to survey questions	Information gathered by mail, phone, email, or web-based surveys, such as customer satisfaction, Net Promoter Score, needs, capabilities, and interests.
Promotion history (outbound marketing communications touches)	The frequency, medium, offer code, cost, and type of your outbound contacts with the account can be helpful in two ways: as a predictor of purchase propensity and as part of a customer value analysis. Response history is also helpful here.
Service history	This includes the contacts the customer has had with your service center, such as inquiries, returns, and problems, plus the resolutions of these communications.
Original source of the contact	In addition to recording where the first contact with this person originated, some companies also include the most recent source of the contact. This second piece of information serves as an indicator of campaign results.
Demographic/firmographic data	In business marketing, the two most powerful predictive variables are industry and company size (defined by revenue or number of employees). But other demographic variables might have value for you, including such factors as the number of sites and the fiscal year (because the business's calendar year is when the budgets close, and open).
Unique identifier	Every record needs a unique identifier. If your data has come from a compiled source, each record will come with an ID. Some systems add sequential ID numbers, and other use a match code type of ID generated from selected characters in the name.

If you are building a database in support of distribution channel partners, your database also includes the elements in Table 3.6.

Table 3.6   Data Fields Used in Channel Partner Databases

Data Elements	Considerations
Type of channel partner	Most companies tier their channel partners based on various criteria, like their special skills and expertise, their performance or the depth of their relationship with the manufacturer. Another way to classify partners is by their business model, whether distributor, manufacturer's representative, or retailer. Or, the partners might be identified by their territory, or the breadth of their market coverage.
Years as partner	The number of years that the channel partner has been associated with the company gives important clues to the business opportunity. For example, newer partners tend to be more aggressive in their sales and marketing efforts, but are often given a less complete product line to start.
Industries served	Not all channel partners are full service. Some might specialize in specific vertical markets. Recognizing industry specialization enables you to align or link customers to partners who specialize in their industries.
Products covered	This data enables you to link SKU and product tables to partners. Not all channel partners carry a full line. Some might specialize in specific technical products, or have limited capability to support a full line. In combination with industry information, this field also enables you to link customers and partners by both industry and product interest.
Territory covered	This identifies the actual geography that is covered by this partner according to their agreement with you. The territory indicator can be defined broadly, such as by country, in the case of a global partner, or as narrowly as by ZIP code for a local channel partner.
Sales rep assigned	This extremely important piece of information identifies the link between the channel partner and the internal sales representative responsible for the relationship. In marketing programs that impact the channel, it is crucial that you get the sales representative's buy-in and support.

Data Hygiene Best Practices

As every B-to-B marketer knows, business data tends to degrade quickly—major understatement. According to Dun & Bradstreet, every year in the United States:

- Business postal addresses on your file change at a rate of 20.7%. If your customer is a new business, the rate is 27.3%.

- Phone numbers change at the rate of 18% overall, and 22.7% among new businesses.

- Company names change at the rate of 12.4% among all companies and a staggering 36.4% among new businesses.

The reason for this massive instability is the volatility of the business world. Also according to D&B, in the United States:

- A new business opens every minute.

- A business closes every 3 minutes.

- A CEO changes every minute.

- A company name change occurs every 2 minutes.

- A new business files for bankruptcy every 8 minutes.

Overall, business data is said to degrade at a rate of 3% to 6% a month, making approximately one-third to three-quarters of it obsolete every year. If fresh data is a valuable asset—and it is a priceless one—dirty data is an enormous liability, leading to

- Undeliverable communications

- False intelligence

- Irritated customers

- An unprofessional image

- A bad reputation

- Lost business opportunity

It's a Dirty Job, But Someone Has to Do It (Probably You)

Luckily, there is a process that keeps your data scrubbed and fresh despite marketplace instability. It's called *data hygiene*, which is defined as "correcting inaccurate fields and standardizing formats and data elements." Instilling data hygiene best practices into your database management takes a commitment of time and resources, but not doing it can degrade your operation to the point of no return.

The data hygiene process has two major parts: entering clean data and then keeping it clean. To achieve these goals, you need to undertake both manual and automated steps. Here is how to avoid the plague of dirty data—like, well, the plague.

Step one is to receive and enter data that is clean in the first place. This involves:

- Data that is entered without clear, consistent, specific guidelines is likely to be a mess. So the first thing you need to do is create a set of rules for data elements known as Input Editing Standards (IES), which must be followed at the point of entry. For instance, a standard requirement is to make state abbreviations conform to the USPS two-digit standards.

- If your company already has a database, there is probably an input standards document kicking around—somewhere. See if you can scout it out, and then review, refresh, and launch it into use. If you can't find it, then you'll have to write one. The IES rules are your bible, so you might want to get some professional help. Refer to USPS Publication 28 for examples of recommended field selection and layout of business addresses. It is available for free download as a PDF, from http://pe.usps.gov/cpim/ftp/pubs/Pub28/pub28.pdf.

B-to-B mailers have many more data elements to be concerned about than the simple three-line consumer address. There are various permutations of firm names, the use of prestige/vanity addresses, auxiliary company, and personnel data; for example, titles—personal/professional and departmental or division, and so on. Moreover, company, contact, distribution, and delivery address information for businesses can be daunting. Therefore, for the B-to-B mailer, the scope of address standardization and list maintenance and correction is quite complex.

The data elements that can be included in a business-to-business address are in Table 3.7.

Distribution and delivery address data elements are the focus of USPS standardization recommendations.

The U.S. Postal Service (USPS) has worked with B-to-B mailers in developing guidelines/standards for address formatting, standard abbreviations, and address compression to help alleviate the following problems that can result in processing B-to-B lists:

- Inefficiencies in the merge/purge process
- Poor address hygiene
- Missed opportunities for barcoding discounts
- Non-deliverability

Table 3.7   USPS Recommendations: Data Hygiene/Standardization

Company and Contact Information	Distribution and Delivery Address Information	
Name prefix	Street number	City
First name	Predirectional	State
Middle name or initial	Street name	ZIP
Surname	Street suffix	ZIP+4
Suffix title	Postdirectional	Carrier route code
Professional title	Secondary unit indicator	Optional endorsement
Functional title	Secondary number	Key line code
Division/department name	Company name	POSTNET barcode
Mailstop code	PO box number	POSTNET address block barcode

Most B-to-B list maintenance companies have adopted the USPS standards as part of their processing procedures. For a quick and easy reference, visit the USPS website (www.usps.com) and search for Publication 28, Postal Addressing Standards. Chapter 3 in Publication 28 focuses on B-to-B addressing.

TRAINING IS KEY TO HYGIENE SUCCESS

Train all key entry personnel in IES rules, with training repeated at least quarterly. Consider naming a small number of data standards specialists to maintain the standards, update them as needed, red-flag any problems and serve as go-to people for the rest of the data-entry personnel.

Also, create standardized lists for such fields as function and level in your database values. This encourages your teams to choose from a predefined list and improves consistency, quality, and accuracy.

Step two is to institute ongoing updating of manual processes. Here is your to-do list for setting up processes to keep your data clean using manual methods:

- Invite your customers to help you maintain their information correctly. Make the contact information available on a password-protected website, and ask your customers to enter changes as they occur. Offer a premium or incentive, or even a discount, to obtain higher levels of compliance. Ask for customer data regularly, and make it easy for the customer to provide the information. Always ask for the information the same way—no matter where you ask for it.

- Train and motivate call center personnel, customer service, salespeople, and distributors—anyone with direct customer contact—to request updated information at each meeting.

- Segment your file, and conduct outbound confirmation contacts for the highest value accounts. This can be by mail, email, or telephone. Decide in advance the acceptable incidence of errors in the record. If that error rate is exceeded, then undertake an outbound communications program by phone and email to update the records. When you have some results, do an analysis to decide whether to put your less valuable accounts through the same process.

- When using first-class mail, request the address correction service provided by the USPS. Put in place a process to update the addresses from the "nixies," meaning the undeliverable mail that is returned to you.

- Pay for postal returns (endorsements) and update your files with the returns. This should be done at least once a year, and ideally two to four times a year. Learn the pros and cons of the different endorsement options and how they operate within both Standard and First Class Mail:

  - Address Change Service (ACS)

  - Address Service Requested

  - Return Service Requested

  - Change Service Requested

  - Forwarding Service Requested

- Check out USPS.com for a wealth of good information and tips on addressing options, including:

  - www.usps.com/businessmail101/addressing/specialAddress.htm

  - www.usps.com/directmail/undeliverablemail.htm

  - www.usps.com/business/addressverification/welcome.htm

Step three involves instituting ongoing updating of automated processes. This helps keep automated processes and customer information clean. Following are the tasks related to this step:

- After you put manual methods in motion, send your data out at least twice a year to be matched against national databases of standardized records. However, be forewarned: All you can count on to be 100% clean are postal addresses, because the USPS is the only ultimate standard for these service providers. The job titles, telephone numbers, fax numbers, and email addresses found in vendor databases will most likely not be any fresher than yours. Unfortunately, you have to verify these manually, through outbound contact and inbound web-based updating.

- Run your house file through the USPS DSF2 (Delivery Sequence File) protocol, which identifies whether an address is a business or a residence. The process enables you to sort out residential "three-line" addresses from real business addresses that are just missing a company name and identify potentially undeliverable business addresses.

Database Analysis, Segmentation, and Modeling

Your data is freshly scrubbed. You have put into place practices to keep it that way. Now your MDB is sitting there, brimful of potential, waiting for its first assignment like the most eager new employee—one that won't ever ask for a minute of time off. What do you want it to do first to launch your lead generation program?

Segmentation and Targeting: Zeroing in on Your Best Bets

One of the most important uses of data is to identify the best potential prospects and select the most appropriate of them to approach with marketing communications. This process is called *targeting*. But before you can target, you need to divide the universe into groups based on certain defining characteristics in another process called *segmentation*.

Segmentation lets you zero in on a group so you can create the most appropriate messages and use the best communications channels, thereby increasing the likelihood of response. It provides segments that can act as small universes for testing and roll out.

Who Makes the Cut? Segmentation Criteria

Although possible segmentation criteria are virtually limitless, you need to apply strict guidelines when you segment. Focus exclusively on creating segments that will be meaningful to your business and that are:

- Large enough in profit potential to be worth it. Ask yourself: Is the segment too narrow to justify the cost of analysis and customization programs?

- Accessible by current sales channels or new ones that can realistically and affordably be established

- Serviceable—for example, your company has the resources and processes in place to manage the ensuing relationship

The following criteria are those most frequently used by business marketers. However, keep in mind that your criteria are fashioned by your own business function and needs.

Relationship

- Customers versus prospects

- Cold prospects versus inquirers

- Repeat customers versus first-time buyers

- Frequent customers versus occasional buyers

- Sales coverage

- Source from which they responded (trade show, seminar, mail, Internet, customer service call, and so on)

- Offer to which they responded

Geographics

- Region, state, metropolitan area, and so on

- Climate

- Proximity to distribution channels or competitors

Demographics (sometimes known as *firmographics*)

- SIC code, or NAICS
- Sales volume
- Number of employees
- Credit rating
- Buyer characteristics (gender, purchasing patterns, style, and so on)
- Buying process and requirements
- Year founded

Purchase history

- Product lines
- Stage in the product life cycle
- RFM (recency, frequency, and monetary value of purchases)
- Competitive purchases

B-to-B marketing databases have many uses across the sales and marketing spectrum. The data in Table 3.8 was collected through the survey from a sample of several hundred marketers ranking their database applications. Notice how lead generation (prospecting, campaign selection, inquiry management, and response tracking) tops the list.

Table 3.8   How B-to-B Marketers Use Their Databases

Answer Options	Response %	Response Count
Marketing to prospects	80.11%	145
Campaign target selection	70.72%	128
Contact or inquiry management	61.33%	111
Query	60.22%	109
Export data (for example, to your mail house, or email vendor, or to a co-op database)	57.46%	104
Campaign response tracking and analysis	44.75%	81
Import data (for example, from in-house sources, like operating system, sales force automation system, or from your website)	44.20%	80
Customer profiling	42.54%	77
Capture data about end-users	36.46%	66

Table 3.8   How B-to-B Marketers Use Their Databases

Answer Options	Response %	Response Count
Perform data hygiene/record deduplication	31.49%	57
Segmentation for product development purposes	29.28%	53
Identify multi-buyers	28.73%	52
Data append or enhancement from 3rd party supplier, like D&B, InfoUSA or Experian	28.18%	51
Campaign strategy planning	27.07%	49
Identify unique buyers at a site	18.78%	34
Lifetime value (LTV) analysis	14.92%	27
RFM	13.26%	24
Modeling to predict campaign response	13.26%	24
Modeling to predict sales or purchase	12.15%	22
Predictive modeling using regression	9.94%	18
Predictive modeling through cluster analysis	8.29%	15
Modeling for winback or reactivation	8.29%	15
Predictive modeling using tree algorithms like CHAID or CART	7.18%	13
Modeling to predict defection	6.63%	12
Other	4.42%	8

Modeling and Analysis: The Power to Predict

After segmentation, lead generators are likely to use their databases to build predictive models. The purpose of a model is to identify the most promising targets for a particular campaign. Modeling is most often done internally on house files. But owners of large lists, especially prospect databases, might offer modeling services in order to help marketers make better selections from their files for prospecting campaigns.

Business files tend to be small but complex, which is why many modeling techniques that work well with high-volume consumer data don't translate to B-to-B. One of the simplest and least expensive database modeling applications in lead generation analytic techniques is penetration analysis. In B-to-B, this usually involves analysis by four-digit, six-digit, or eight-digit SIC against a national master file of businesses. When you compare the SICs of your customer file against the whole market, you can get a good feel for where your strength lies in the marketplace, industry by industry. A high penetration rate generally indicates success in that industry sector, suggesting that additional efforts there will pay off.

Another modeling application widely practiced in B-to-B is using cluster analysis, or its more sophisticated cousin, CHAID. Clustering enables you to separate your file into groups of like characteristics, and can be used effectively with relatively small files:

- **Cluster analysis.** Clustering finds groupings based on a variety of variables—for example, company size, industry and purchase patterns. Cluster analysis of your best customers can help identify the characteristics you should be looking for when prospecting.

- **Chi-Square Automatic Interaction Detector (CHAID).** A kind of "tree algorithm" that develops statistically significant groupings of records based on behaviors, such as response or payment.

One of modeling's biggest benefits to business marketers is its capability to help you separate and rank. Models can help you determine the data elements with the most positive and negative impact on sales results. They can also build a predictive, ranked list of who is important in buying what—particularly significant in the complex world of B-to-B, in which buying roles tend to change by product. For instance, the tech specifications person might be the most important in electronic equipment, while the purchasing agent makes the decision for office furniture. Build good models and you can target your marketing communications accordingly, ringing the doorbells that lead to ringing up sales.

The kind of information modeling delivers is worth a lot—but it will also cost you. Plan on spending at least $20,000 to build a model, and plan on redoing your model at least once a year.

PROFILING: PICTURING PROSPECTS AS CUSTOMERS

An excellent way to select the right prospect segments is to compare them by key characteristics to your customer base. Predictive characteristics can include industry, company size (extrapolated from number of employees), company revenues, and geographic territory. The idea is that if you select prospects similar to your best customers, they will similarly want to do business with you. Just make sure that the selection characteristics chosen can lead to a list you can actually service.

For example, say your best customers are those who prefer to buy through a certain class of distributors. It's unlikely that you will be able to find media channels, such as mailing lists, that deliver buyers with that particular characteristic. In this case, you need to come up with another, more actionable, criterion.

4

Campaign Development Best Practices

As you begin planning your lead-generation campaigns, it's a good idea to keep an eye on emerging developments. Thanks to experimentation on the part of business-to-business (B-to-B) marketers and their willingness to share results, we can all learn from new best practices as they come to light. This chapter discusses three examples that have proven themselves: research and testing, content marketing, and marketing automation. Each of them is now making a strong contribution to lead-generation success.

Best Practice I: Research and Testing

You have set your campaign objectives, determined your lead flow needs, and analyzed your customers' buying processes. You may have even created a preliminary campaign budget. Now it is time to consider how to take advantage of research and testing to increase the likelihood of your campaign's success.

The first step in campaign development usually involves research. Pre-campaign research should be used to confirm target audience selection, identify the strongest offers and message platforms, and otherwise narrow down as much as possible the myriad variables that go into campaign planning decisions. Most pre-campaign research is done using quantitative and qualitative methods to understand customer needs and preferences.

Testing, on the other hand, involves peeling off a sample of the audience, and actually running a campaign—or particular portions of the campaign—to that sample. After results are understood, then either the winning elements of the test are rolled out as a campaign to the rest of the audience or the elements are sent back to the drawing board to identify opportunities for improvement. In summary, research and testing can reduce the risk of making sub-optimal marketing investments, so they are both highly recommended as a standard part of lead-generation planning and execution.

Qualitative and Quantitative Pre-Campaign Research

Compared to consumer direct-response communications, where most research takes the form of in-market testing, lead generation makes considerable use of primary research. There are a number of good reasons for this:

- Business target universes are small—often representing fewer than 10,000 accounts—and cannot support numerous test cells with statistical validity.

- Each business prospect can represent significant value, so any technique that allows the campaign to penetrate the universe more deeply is usually worth doing. Pre-campaign research falls into this category.

- Campaign budgets—and expected revenue outcomes—usually support the expense of pre-campaign research.

Pre-campaign research falls into two buckets:

1. **Qualitative research, involving in-depth questions and answers.**
   Types of qualitative research include focus groups, one-on-one in-depth interviews and open-ended mail, email, or phone surveys. The best uses of qualitative research in lead generation are

- Validate assumptions about buyer motivation.

- Present sample message platforms and creative treatments to get directional reactions.

- Delve into the rational and emotional triggers of various buyer types.

- Develop a deeper understanding of the customer's point of view.

- Gather phrases for copywriting purposes.

- Compare the relative attractiveness of key benefits and features.

2. **Quantitative research, involving statistically valid samples to represent the entire universe.** Quantitative research is usually performed through surveys—whether using telephone, email, or postal mail—to a projectable number of respondents. Quantitative research can be used to validate hypotheses around any critical campaign variable. For lead-generation campaigns, quantitative research is often used to assess

- The best potential offers

- List segments or list quality

- Purchase intent

- Product awareness

- Message preferences

- Creative concept rankings

- Improvements in your control package

- Willingness to participate in further research

Some business marketers value research so much that they find it productive to set up ongoing panels of customers and prospects who have agreed to answer questions on a regular basis. Panels can be relatively large to provide statistical reliability, or they can be small, the way a focus group is. They can be managed by postal mail, email, or at a website. The advantage of panels is the steady, consistent source of feedback they provide, and the fact that they keep respondent recruitment expenses low.

Testing to Improve Lead-Generation Campaign Results

As mentioned previously, testing is a valuable way to enhance the productivity of your lead-generation campaigns and reduce the risk of low performance. However, the small size of most target marketing in B-to-B means that testing isn't quite as smooth a road as it can be in the consumer sector. Truth is, there are plenty of pot-holes that argue against testing. For one thing, the logistics of test and control in the multi-touch, long-sales-cycle world of B-to-B can be daunting. It's often too tough to set up a control group for so many variables. For another, your sales force may balk at the idea of some customers receiving different messages or offers from other customers—especially because, in B-to-B, there are often multiple customers in the same company. Furthermore, testing incurs a certain extra amount of expense, so some marketers are reluctant to pursue testing when the dollars could go directly to campaigning.

 Tip

Even if the sales force is resistant to testing, keep them in the loop. You risk major damage to relationships and morale by testing into their territo-ries and taking them by surprise.

Despite the drawbacks, testing is still worth your serious consideration. There's too big a potential payoff to let the pitfalls scare you away, and a well planned pre-testing and research program can give you a leg up, not only in terms of market penetration, but also against your competition.

Keep these guidelines in mind as you develop your testing plan:

- **Test only what's important.** It's only natural for marketers to want to know everything about their customers and prospects, but resist the temptation to ask random questions just because the results may be interesting. Limit your tests to variables that can make a substantial economic difference when they are rolled out.

- **Be creative about testing options.** For instance, if you are working with a compiled list of prospects and you have no other list to test it against, telephone or email a few names to get an early sense of the list's quality.

- **Test an offer in every campaign.** Offer testing can have sizable lever-age, and it will be helpful to have an archive of tested offers whenever you need them—say, for inquiry generation or lead nurturing.

- **Find new routes to your best prospects.** If you have a responsive audi-ence, see if you can make them respond even more with a different approach. If a trade publication ad pulls well, try renting the mailing list. If you are mailing a segment successfully, test telephoning them.

- **Test into your strengths.** If a list works well, test additional selects on it. If you have a strong offer, test variations against it.

- **Use less-expensive media.** Limit your risks and keep costs in line by split testing headlines and offers with cheaper media such as email and banner ads.

Ten Ways to Manage Campaign Risk

When you can't do pure testing with statistically projectable samples to provide reliable predictions of campaign results, one alternative is to adjust your expectations, accept an increased amount of risk, and then seek ways to mitigate that risk. Here are ten tips that can help, all of them endorsed by direct marketing statisticians and experts:

1. **Lower the confidence level required for your tests.** Mark Klein, CEO of Loyalty Builders LLC, points out that reducing your expected confidence level from direct marketing's traditional 90–95 percent to the 60 percent range can make dramatically smaller test quantities productive, or at least directional. "This kind of testing, while more prone to error, still improves your chances of hitting a winner with a small target universe," says Klein, "which is the whole point."

THE MATH BEHIND REDUCING CONFIDENCE LEVEL REQUIREMENTS

Say you have a universe of 2,000 email addresses. You send out two different emails to two equal segments of 1,000 each and produce responses of 7 percent and 10 percent, respectively. Is the 10 percent side of the split a true winner or just a random error?

According to Bill Vorias, a mathematician with Loyalty Builders, 72 percent of the time, this result represents a significant difference. Not 95 percent, but not bad. To get to 90 percent confidence in this situation, you'd need a sample size of roughly 1,700 for each group, or 3,400 for the campaign. Or, looking at it from the other direction, if you only have 2,500 email addresses to play with, you'd have to be satisfied with an 80 percent confidence that the difference is meaningful.

For anyone who wants to reproduce these numbers, Vorias says you need to know that this was at an alpha level of 0.05 and it was a one-sided (versus two-sided) test.

2. **Campaign sequentially.** Running campaigns to the same audience over
    time replicates the results you would expect from a split test. The risk
    lies in the introduction of time as a variable. However, says Andrew
    Drefahl, director of customer insight and technology at Hunter
    Business Group, "Rapid iteration becomes a learning process. You learn
    by failure, developing rules of thumb you can then apply to other cam-
    paign situations."

3. **Make reasonable assumptions.** Take what works in one medium, such
    as the phone, and make the assumption that it also works in the mail or
    in email.

4. **Test at the contact level, but read results at the site level.** Andrew
    Drefahl suggests expanding your universe by testing at the contact level
    and reading at the site level. Conduct your campaign to multiple con-
    tacts in an account, and then measure campaign success in aggregate by
    how well the account as a whole accepts your value proposition, instead
    of measuring the results for each contact. Drefahl recommends using
    the phone to measure this acceptance, or "uptake," so you can probe the
    motivating factors behind the response. "It's the test-and-learn
    approach, which is often the only way to open doors in a small B-to-B
    audience," he says.

A TESTING TOOL FOR SMALL UNIVERSES

The "Power Test," pioneered by the Hacker Group, provides a methodology
for generating a control direct-mail package from scratch using only 50,000
names. Essentially, the Power Test suspends the need for each test cell to be
statistically projectable on its own, but lets you read results in aggregate
across several lists. This way, with only two test runs of 25,000 each, a control package can be culled from two offer tests, three creative tests, and five
or more test lists.

5. **Swipe successful ideas from others.** Jim Obermayer, founder of the
    Sales Lead Management Association, suggests following the lead of
    direct marketing creative directors, many of whom maintain a "swipe
    file" of competitive control ads they see repeatedly. "If your competition
    has figured out what's working, why not reap some benefit from the
    other guy's investment?" asks Obermayer.

6. **Strengthen your offer.** Business people love freebies, and new gizmos and gadgets are coming on the market all the time. Keep close contact with premium vendors so you can be the first to offer the hottest new item. "Remember those little electric fans a few years back, where the brand name was spelled out in the air via electrodes?" says Obermayer. "Everyone had to have one." Even if you can't test, you are at least giving your campaign its best shot.

7. **Use your house file, which is your list of current customers and inquirers.** As Stephen R. Lett, president of Lett Direct, points out, "The higher response rate from your house file gets you closer to reliable testing with a smaller universe. You can then take these results and apply them to your prospecting campaigns. It's not perfect, but it's better than not testing at all."

8. **Think big.** You'll get more bang for the buck by testing more powerful creative offers than you will by seeking cost savings. Lee Marc Stein, a veteran copywriter, suggests testing your way from envelope mail to a dimensional package, or moving from a #10 to a #14 mail piece.

9. **Swing for the fences.** Lee Marc Stein also recommends testing only the changes likely to have the most impact. With small universes, you can't test nuances.

10. **Optimize your web-based response forms.** Thanks to free tools like the Website Optimizer in Google Analytics, marketers can set up multiple types of tests on critical web pages such as registration forms, order forms, and landing pages—anywhere that a response is requested.

TRY AN ENTERPRISE-WIDE CONTROL GROUP

The enterprise-wide control group, advocated by Richard N. Tooker, author of *The Business of Database Marketing*, enables a company to set up a single control group for multiple campaigns over time by establishing an ongoing, standard control group made up of, say, 5 percent of the customer base. The purpose of the corporate control group, which receives no marketing communications at all, is to assess the value of the direct marketing program as a whole. But, it may also be used as a benchmark for particular campaigns, if the campaign goes to the entire balance of the universe. Just keep in mind: Tooker cautions that if the campaign is going out to a smaller segment, the portion of the corporate control group that is comparable may quickly become too small to be valid.

Best Practice II: The New Importance of Content Marketing

Call it custom publishing, call it custom media, call it content marketing—what you call it doesn't matter, but relevant, valuable content in print, digital, audio, or visual formats—or all of the above—is the new must-have for B-to-B marketers. Your customers are clamoring for it, and your competitors are dishing it up as fast as they can.

Odds are, your company is already there. According to a 2010 joint study of 1,100 business marketers conducted by Junta42 and MarketingProfs, nine out of ten organizations have content marketing initiatives in place, and they are spending significant sums and planning to spend even more. Respondents reported allocating about 26 percent of their budgets to content, and more than half of those surveyed planned to increase that amount over the next 12 months. (A 2009 survey from the Custom Publishing Council puts the percentage spent on content marketing even higher at 32 percent.)

Content marketing is serving an important need that has emerged from the Internet's enormous impact on the way business people buy today. Instead of calling in vendors to help them analyze and develop solutions to their problems, buyers today are going online and researching problems for themselves.

Consider this data from GlobalSpec, the industrial market search engine company, which researched the sources industrial buyers are using to get educated. As seen in Table 4.1, the top three sources used today are online. Your prospects are there, so you need to be there, too.

If business buyers are not talking to sales people until later in the buy cycle, this means that marketers must get into the act, in a big way. The result is the new discipline of content marketing, whereby marketers develop an array of educational materials, made available online and elsewhere, and designed to gain important influence in the early stages of the buying process. This content is intended *not only* to educate and demonstrate thought leadership, but also to steer the prospect toward your solution.

But effective content is not just any collateral that you have lying around. You want to provide content that goes way beyond mere "information." The best marketing content is customized to soothe pain points and make buyers look smart. It delivers relevant advice that helps them do their jobs and provides the in-depth knowledge they need to make a buying decision.

Table 4.1   Sources Used by Business Buyers to Research Solutions

Source Used When Searching for Products/Services to Purchase	Mean Score on a Scale of 1–7; 1 = Rarely Use and 7 = Always Use
Search engines	5.6
Supplier websites	5.5
Online catalogs	4.9
Colleagues	4.3
Printed catalogs	4.1
Printed trade publications	3.2
Printed directories	3.1
Online industry portal sites	3.0
Trade shows/conferences	2.8
E-newsletters	2.5
White papers	2.3
Online communities	2.2
Other B-to-B vertical search engines	2.1
Webcasts/webinars	2.0
Social media	1.4

Source: Understanding the Industrial Buy Cycle, GlobalSpec, 2010

Paul Gillin, B-to-B social media expert commentator, puts it this way: "...marketers will no longer be able to push empty messages, because they will simply be ignored. The only hope for marketing is to become a valued source of advice. That doesn't mean publishing more promotional white papers. It means listening to the market and helping customers make wiser decisions, even if that means recommending someone else's product."

According to Globalspec, buyers examine more than six pieces of content before making a decision about large purchases. Your company should build a library of content assets that can serve different needs.

In B-to-B marketing today, the leading formats for content marketing include

- Archived webinars
- Blog entries
- Case studies
- Podcasts

- Research reports

- Video demos and testimonials

- White papers

 Tip

Today, not having a blog is like not having a phone. A recent Ivy Worldwide study showed that when CEOs purchase technology, they do exactly what you and I do—they search Google, they look for customer reviews and testimonials, and then they buy. Google loves blogs because they're fresh and relevant. Lots of small businesses use the WordPress platform to construct their web sites. It's mostly free and easy to customize.

How to Develop Winning Content

To make your company's content initiatives stand out from the pack, follow these guidelines adapted from Junta42's Content Marketing Institute:

- **Narrow your focus.** Content that's a "mile wide and an inch deep" won't make it. You need materials that zero in on your customers' needs and problems. Content marketing is not one-size-fits-all.

- **Know your audience.** The best way to narrow your focus is by knowing your audience intimately. Make their focus your focus. HR managers have different needs than inventory managers. Imagine your buyer pulling out your content as a reference at an important meeting or presentation. Create something quotable.

- **What's your point?** What do you want readers to take away? If your product solves a problem, explain how in detail. If it saves time and money, demonstrate how much. Lose the bloat and buzzwords and stay on message, but keep the focus on problems and solutions, *not* on pitching your product.

- **Share the wealth.** When it comes to your company's products and services, you're in the catbird's seat. You know more about their benefits and features than anyone. Use this insider information about your product or service category to give your readers specific, unique advice and fresh ideas. Don't be afraid that sharing your wealth of information will eliminate the need for your product or service. Instead, your knowhow will actually build your credibility and keep you top of mind when vendors are being identified.

- **Generate action.** Buyers are busy. Make sure your content includes actionable ideas—ones that can be implemented immediately.

- **Sell, but oh-so-softly.** These are marketing materials and they need a marketing purpose. Your customers will be okay with that, if you do it right. Eight out of ten respondents in the Junta42/Marketing Profs survey said they didn't mind sponsor selling, as long as the information was interesting. One way to soft sell is to outline the characteristics, features, and specifications your customers should seek when shopping in your category. In short, you are educating them about how to be a knowledgeable buyer. Then, make it easy to match them up with the product or service you're selling.

- **Go deep, but don't pull them under.** Your content should be in-depth but not daunting. Leave out the stuff they don't need and summarize the content. You can always follow up with links for readers who want more. "Extraneous detail adds length without adding detail," says Bob Bly, noted copywriter and Internet specialist. "Leave it out."

- **Don't be afraid to be likeable.** People buy from other people they like and trust. Write about challenges you have overcome and improvements you've made to your product or service, announce new things, and promote events.

The Junta42/Marketing Profs survey shows that marketers are using a variety of content tactics or types. Table 4.2 lists the top ten.

Table 4.2   Ten Top Content Tactics

Tactic	Percentage Using
Social media (excluding blogs)	79
Articles	78
In-person events	62
eNewsletters	61
Case studies	55
Blogs	51
White papers	43
Webinars/Webcasts	42
Print magazines	42
Videos	41

WHAT'S AHEAD IN CONTENT MARKETING

It's an exciting time to be in content marketing, a field that is evolving quickly. B-to-B marketers are beginning to realize they need to develop an entire content marketing strategy, beginning with an inventory of content "assets," and a strategic look at the stages in the buying cycles and the needs of the various parties involved in the buying circle—all the way to the deliberate creation of content needed to create a comprehensive library of relevant material that is available to influence buyers across the board.

Some of the latest developments in content marketing are in the areas of mobile and video. The Content Marketing Institute recommends that mobile applications be fully integrated into your content marketing plan. They suggest that you think of ways to target your customers with content via their mobile devices, and look into getting a .mobi extension for your website.

According to the Nielsen rating service, 90 percent of all web traffic will be video by 2013. If you want to be found, you must use video. Consider video interviews, demonstrations, and training on how to use your product or service. Set up a branded YouTube channel and send customers there for more information. Post videos on the YouTube channel and embed them into your blog.

Content Resources You Should Know

As you consider how to include content marketing as part of your lead-generation program, plenty of resources are available to help you, among them:

- **MarketingProfs.com.** This includes a library of articles, seminars, and cases, the bulk of them relevant to B-to-B marketing.

- **MarketingSherpa.com.** This includes weekly case studies and research, with sections for both business and consumer audiences.

- **RainToday.com.** This site offers resources for marketers of professional services.

- **CMI (ContentMarketingInstitute.com).** CMI provides thought leadership on content development and usage.

- **WhichTestWon.com.** This site has examples of split test results from real campaigns.

Best Practice III: Marketing Automation

It's fairly obvious now that the B-to-B buying process has changed. One way to describe it is that business buyers act more like consumers. They're using the wealth of information available online and through social networks to shop around, research products, and research vendors. That means they may not be ready to talk to a sales rep, even on the phone, until they've already decided to purchase.

With salespeople involved later, marketers must be involved earlier, keeping customers and prospects warm with a steady stream of educational content and relationship-building until they're ready for a sales call. This is why content marketing has come to the fore. This also explains the need for marketing-automation tools, to make this extended nurturing part of the process more efficient and effective.

Marketing automation systems are also a huge benefit for tracking, which is traditionally tricky in business marketing. It is now possible to design automated multi-step email campaigns to track responses at a detailed level, including monitoring website visits and tracking sales back to specific campaigns. Tools like this help you better define a campaign's ROI and its contribution to sales.

You can use automation as extensively or minimally as you like, from simple email execution to web-based automated multichannel marketing campaigns. Table 4.3 shows just a few representative tasks currently able to be automated, along with where they fit into the sales cycle:

Table 4.3   How Automation Enables Lead Generation Processes

Marketing Activity	What Automation Can Do
Campaign measurement and management	Develop response forms and landing pages in one platform.
	Automate event processes, such as invitations, registration and follow-up communications.
	Nurture prospects and customers with automated trigger-based drip campaigns.
Response management	Capture leads with "smart" forms that recognize known visitors.
Inquiry management	Convert web traffic into leads.
	Automate sales tasks and follow-up tracking.
Lead nurturing	Trigger relevant responses to prospect behaviors.
	Manage your content asset library.
Lead scoring	Score leads using demographics and behaviors.
	Automate lead qualification processes.

continued

Table 4.3   How Automation Enables Lead Generation Processes (continued)

Marketing Activity	What Automation Can Do
Lead routing	Capture and assign leads, ensuring that the sales force gets the right information to convert more opportunities.
Content management	Store, distribute, and track content.
	Upload and manage documents and image files.
	Track which pieces are viewed by prospects and notify sales reps whenever key assets are viewed.
Lead database management	Maintain bi-directional synchronization with your CRM system.
Marketing results analytics and measurement	Report on marketing program effectiveness and ROI.

A 2009 study from Forrester Research, commissioned by SilverPop, found lead generation to be the number one reason marketers value automation tools, as you see in Table 4.4. Respondents were asked, "What primary benefits did you gain from marketing automation?"

Table 4.4   Marketers Value Automation Tools for Lead Generation

Benefit	Number of Respondents
Better leads, more robust pipeline	9
Greater visibility into marketing activities	7
Better customer insight/data	7
Efficiency	4
Improved marketing accountability	3

Automation Vendors: Who You Gonna Call?

You'll have no problem finding a vendor to supply the automation system your company needs. Forrester Research recently placed SAS and Unica at the top of their recommended list, with others—including Eloqua, Marketo, and Pardot—setting industry standards and growing fast. These vendors develop software specific to campaign management, lead nurturing, triggered marketing communications, and more, resulting in applications for virtually every phase of the B-to-B sales cycle. Signs are that even more applications will become available as we go forward.

Have a look at a variety of vendors, including the following:

- Alterian
- Aprimo
- Eloqua
- Genius
- InfusionSoft
- LeadLife
- Manticore Technology
- MarketBright

- Neolane
- Net-Results
- NurtureHQ
- Pardot
- Responsys
- SAS
- Silverpop
- Unica

Marketing automation is quickly gaining traction with B-to-B marketers, as evidenced by a 2010 Marketing Sherpa study. A reported 54 percent of CMO respondents said they had either begun or completed their implementation of some kind of marketing automation software, and another 17 percent say they intend to implement. The challenges of meeting the lead-generation imperative without automation are simply too great.

Case Study: When the Chips Were Down, Marketing Got Automated

One excellent example of how marketing automation can be used for lead generation can be found in the case of AMD, a $4.6 billion computer chip maker in Austin, TX. Marketing Manager Ann Fatino's team developed a program using a series of outbound email communications to the end users of their product: the consumers and businesses who bought the computers (from such manufacturers as IBM, Gateway, and Dell) driven by AMD's chips. Fatino's program was customized both to refer to the content of each inquirer's responses to previous messages and to capture new information for future messaging.

The AMD team was able to identify plenty of meaningful message variables: their preferred computer brand, the evaluation criteria they use in the purchase decision, and, no surprise, incentive messages that triggered action. All good, but the more data points gathered, the more complicated the process became. The team decided automation was the way to go and hired a local agency, Oak Sanderson, to come up with a solution.

Oak Sanderson built an application that resulted in an end-to-end lead management system capable of sorting inquiries by various qualification criteria and then separating them into three categories, according to how soon and how much they were planning to buy:

- "Hot" leads went directly to business development, to be sorted by sales reps. Weekly notifications of new leads were sent out to reps, who could log on to obtain the prospect's contact information. The system also allowed the reps to update the account status as they worked the lead, providing the marketing team a clear picture of the situation.

- "Warm" leads went into the customized outbound email process, where data points from the original inquiry were evaluated. Then, a series of customized email communications was generated, each building on the last, until the prospect indicated readiness to buy within the next six months.

- "Cold" inquiries went through a double process of outbound personalized email communications, in hopes they would warm up and become hot. If not, they were returned to the marketing database for re-promotion.

From its beginnings as a small pilot, the system is now used for inquiries from all sources, trade shows, seminars, advertising, online sources and direct mail campaigns. AMD has a marketing automation success story on its hands.

5

Campaign Media Selection

Put a few business-to-business (B-to-B) marketers together in a room and ask them to name the best lead-generation campaign medium. Then settle back. You may be there awhile. One person will claim direct mail is best because targeted lists are so widely available. Another will staunchly advocate trade shows, where both customers and prospects are likely to be in attendance. Still others, attracted by the rock-bottom cost per contact, prefer email. And of course the telephone—so flexible and personal—will get a lot of votes.

The truth is that each medium has its strengths, weaknesses, and best applications. Your campaign must carefully harness the right medium for each job, factoring in such variables as:

- The cost of each medium
- The medium's availability
- The campaign's time horizon
- Your business objectives

The best answer to the question about the best medium is, "It depends." Plus, because of the long, complex sales cycle in B-to-B marketing, the best medium is often not just one, but a mix of multiple media, used simultaneously or deployed sequentially for multiple touches.

As you consider the most effective medium for lead generation, keep in mind that new media channels emerge all the time, that buyer media consumption is changing quickly, and it's an ongoing challenge for marketers to stay on top of the changing media landscape. A 2009 study by Marketing Sherpa illustrates these changes, as shown in Table 5.1. Technology buyers reported dramatic differences in their media preferences in a mere six-month period. They are eager for information and finding it in a variety of online sources.

Table 5.1   Changing Use of Information Resources by Technology Buyers in the Past Six Months

Medium	Percent Decreasing Use	Percent Increasing Use
Virtual events/virtual tradeshows	−12%	30%
Search engines	−7%	30%
Business news/info websites	−9%	29%
Vendor websites	−8%	29%
Research/analyst	−9%	25%
Technology B2B websites	−11%	24%
Social media (blogs and social networks)	−12%	24%
Newsletters	−16%	15%
Vendor-delivered email	−17%	15%
Face-to-face events/trade shows	−37%	12%
Video programming	−14%	10%
Advertising	−18%	9%

Source: Marketing Sherpa and TechWeb Business Technology Buyer Survey

There are more than a dozen types of outbound campaign media, some tried-and-true and some new. For a handy chart summarizing the media options, see Table 5.5 at the end of this chapter. Whether prospecting media are used solo or in combination, there's no question that some work better for B-to-B lead generation than others. This chapter looks at the cream of the crop and the bottom of the barrel.

B-to-B Lead Generation Media: The Top Five

The cream of the crop in lead generation media consists of five tried-and-true options: telephone, direct mail, search engine marketing (SEM), your website, and trade shows, but only if they attract a large number of prospective buyers. Let's look at each of these key prospect marketing media.

Outbound Telemarketing

The telephone is the Swiss Army knife in the B-to-B marketer's backpack: a flexible, personal, dependable resource with infinite applications. According to the Direct Marketing Association's 2009–2010 *Power of Direct Marketing* study, B-to-B direct marketers spent $15.2 billion in 2010 on telephone marketing for lead generation. That compares to $6.5 billion spent on direct mail and $3.9 billion for search marketing for the same purpose. Were those big bucks worth it? Definitely! The same study reports that the phone generated $193.3 billion in revenue for phone-based lead generation and $106.1 billion in merchandise sales.

One reason for the phone's consistent powerhouse performance is its unique capability to replicate a face-to-face selling environment without the expense of a physical sales call. Early in the sales cycle, the phone makes a great tool for "data discovery" to identify the right contacts or to verify address and title.

HOW TO GET THE MOST VALUE FROM VOICE MAIL MARKETING

Outbound telemarketing is a powerful part of B-to-B sales and marketing, but, as we all know, business people are harder to reach than ever. The net is that 85 percent of calls these days are going to go to voice mail or otherwise not connect. This can be frustrating, but it also offers an opportunity to turn voice mail from an enemy into a friend.

Your campaign strategy needs to be built around your objectives with the outbound call. For example, if you are trying to have a live conversation and you reach a voice mail box, then you should plan on either hanging up or leaving a short voice mail message. The message should request a callback and give a good reason why the prospect should want to talk to you. If, on the other hand, your call is an extra touch to support, say, an event invitation or an email campaign, then you should pre-record the voice mail message and seek to deliver it to every voice mail box on your list.

Here are the elements of best-practice voice mail marketing for lead generation.

- **Plan for multiple outcomes.** Set up your program to be flexible and responsive to whatever happens on the other end of the call. Be ready for either a live conversation or a voice mail message, with both scripts and pre-recorded messages on hand. In other words, prepare for 100 percent message delivery.

- **No wasted calls.** If you're investing in making the call, you want each dial to work as hard as it can. Use a call center that can take advantage of all the options:

  - Navigate pre-recorded messages into voice mail boxes.

  - Conduct a meaningful conversation with a live prospect— whether it's to gather information, probe for a potential lead, modify a data record, or whatever.

  - Transfer a live prospect directly to your sales team.

  - Deliver a hot lead to sales via email.

- **Script adjustment on the fly.** One of the most powerful things about the phone is its flexibility. So, smart marketers take advantage with frequent script refinement in response to positive or negative feedback. "The input we get from our call center's ongoing experience becomes valuable market insight for us," notes Sean Shea, of Expert Server Group.

- **Move fast.** The flexibility of the phone also allows quick turn-on/turn-off—unparalleled in any other medium. By using the new technology platforms, templates and data clean-up processes, you should be able to be on the phone within 24 hours.

- **Inspect often.** Telephone marketing permits instant feedback, so keep a close eye on results, so you can continuously optimize your program. For early stage campaigns, inspect at least daily. For ongoing programs, inspect weekly. "We provide free, fast, and frequent reports to our clients, and we recommend that they look at the top line results but also dive into the detailed call logs, so they can really know what's going on," says Cesario Correia, president of Voicelogic.com in Toronto.

- **Integrate your voice mail program.** Voice mail is part of a larger set of communications strategies, so think about it in the larger context. The easiest way to execute integrated voice mail is by using a call center that provides multiple services under one roof. Look for offerings such as live conversation, hot or live transfer, voice broadcast, fax broadcast, and email delivery, so you can choose the best combination for your campaigns.

- **Craft your voice mail messages.** The secret is to make the message sound real, and not to exceed 30 seconds. This is a personal medium, so think conversation, not advertising. "I've learned over the years to tailor my conversation to sound natural and unscripted, which gives me the best results," says John Price, a long-time rep at Voicelogic.com.

- **Use the latest automation tools.** These days, marketers can order up call center services instantly, using a web-based interface, to give instructions about the campaign details—start date, script, medium, and so forth—and accessing regular reports online. The tools also allow you to repeat a successful campaign with ease and accuracy.

Direct Mail

Direct mail, for decades the workhorse of direct response communications for lead generation, still delivers the goods. The DMA's 2010 *Response Rate Study* reported a healthy 1.68 percent response rate to B-to-B prospecting letter mail and 2.18 percent to its cheaper cousin, postcard mail (see Table 5.2). With 18,500 business lists available for rent in the U.S., most prospective business buyers can be found through the mail, even for obscure products or targeted niches. Business buyers themselves are looking for information to help them do their jobs, and they generally welcome—and open—letters.

Table 5.2   Response Rate Benchmarks Reported by B-to-B Marketers

Direct Mail Format	Response Rate with Customers and Inquirers (House File)	Response Rate with Prospects	Cost Per Lead
Letter-sized envelope	4.28%	1.68%	$135.56
Postcard	4.57%	2.18%	$99.51
Oversized envelope	2.88%	1.20%	$268.08
Dimensional	8.51%	5.11%	$244.00
Catalog	5.44%	0.90%	$45.71

Source: The DMA 2010 Response Rate Report

Business mailers generally prefer enveloped mail, whether it is inside a #10 business size envelope or 6 x 9 inch or larger package. The standard elements of a consumer direct-mail package (outer envelope, letter, brochure, reply form, business reply envelope [BRE]) work solidly for lead generation, but within the category is *dimensional*—also known as "lumpy"—mail, which is often delivered by an express mail service and has special pull. Its high perceived value and standout physical features give it the power to bypass gatekeepers such as mailroom personnel and administrative assistants, allowing it to make its way straight to the executive suite.

According to Spyro Kourtis, president of the direct marketing agency the Hacker Group, a recent mailing to healthcare and financial executives using dimensional mail pulled 12 percent to 15 percent response rates, an outstanding penetration of an otherwise highly resistant audience.

Search Engine Marketing

Business buyers today use the Internet as their primary research tool to solve business problems, so search engine marketing (SEM) has become the hottest of the hot. The medium is highly targeted, with marketers able to bid on search keywords. The risk is acceptable because most SEM opportunities are offered on a pay-per-click basis.

One of the most interesting twists in SEM is the opportunity found in specialized search engines that concentrate on certain industry verticals, such as IT, retailing, or industrial categories. Instead of relying entirely on Google's AdWords and other big players, business marketers are adding directories like GlobalSpec (engineering), BitPipe (IT), goWholesale (retailing), ThomasNet (industrial), and Business.com (general business) to their marketing mix.

Keyword bidding with vertical search engines often results in a better ROI, because verticals deliver a more qualified prospect, who will better convert to a qualified lead. However, this all comes at a price. Your volume is going to be smaller and price per click is likely to be higher. For example, for the term "database software," a #1 ad position on Business.com was priced at $2.10 recently, whereas it cost $1.25 on Google. Businesses are likely to use a mixture of horizontal (general) and vertical search engines—perhaps 25 percent general engines and 75 percent verticals—to deliver the best quality leads at the lowest price.

A couple of caveats about SEM: Due to aggressive competition, this kind of marketing requires constant attention. Also, if people do not search in your category, you're up a creek. Of course, you want to combine your SEM (paid advertising) with search engine optimization (SEO) (copywriting at your website to enhance the likelihood of showing up on search engines) for maximum results.

A NEW TRICK: BANNER AD TARGETING BY DOMAIN NAME

Most banner ad targeting relies on online behavioral indicators like the keyword the visitors are searching on, the content they are looking at, or the pages they visited in the past, as recorded by cookies. Unless you persuade the visitors to disclose their personal information, there's not much else a marketer can do to focus the message.

In the B-to-B world, however, additional tools are available for ad targeting. A website visitor using an office computer, for example, can be identified by company based on the corporate domain name. Sophisticated B-to-B website publishers have been quick to offer targeted ad serving based on company name.

The consulting giant Accenture is already taking advantage of this capability, which is now offered by a variety of leading B-to-B publishers, such as the online editions of *Forbes*, *Businessweek*, and *The Wall Street Journal*.

Because Accenture tends to serve companies no smaller than the Fortune 1000, they constantly seek highly targeted vehicles for their outbound marketing communications in order to avoid waste. Domain name ad serving fits the bill perfectly.

To promote outsourcing deals worth $5 to $10 million among the top 100 electronics and technology corporations, Accenture's communications and high tech practice had a target list of a mere 30 to 50 potential clients. Marten G. van Pelt, marketing director for the practice, provided his prospect list to several business sites, who then served up the Accenture outsourcing ad only when visitors from those top companies appeared.

"We got great results from this campaign," says van Pelt. "We negotiated a CPM, or a flat fee, and of course the cost was higher than normal ad serving, but we had 100 percent control of the targeting and zero waste. I'd say this kind of targeting is worth it, no matter what the price."

Forbes.com's chief advertising officer, Bill Flatley, advises, "The best use of domain name targeting is 'surgical' targeting in concert with a broader campaign." Flatley relates the example of a consulting company involved in a multimillion-dollar systems-integration request for proposal (RFP) that ran ads specific to their systems-integration expertise when visitors showed up at the Forbes site from that prospective client company. Forbes.com charges about a 100 percent premium for the service. Flatley says the biggest users of the option, other than consulting firms, are technology firms and auto leasing companies.

Your Website

You may not have considered this, but the source of your cheapest and most qualified sales leads is right at your fingertips: your company website. Business marketers sometimes tend to see their company's website as just a passive, informational tool—sort of a virtual brochure. Many sites do fit that profile, but you can, and should, add functionality at your site to motivate visitors to leave behind contact information, using an offer and a call to action.

You need a registration area accessible from the home page and ideally included on other pages throughout the site. Use welcoming, benefit-oriented copy supported with a compelling offer, such as a downloadable case study or white paper. Make the registration form as simple or detailed as you want, keeping in mind that asking for more information will likely lower the response but yield better qualified prospects.

It's important to test the number and nature of the questions you ask, because buyer behavior is so different across industries and job functions—and might change over time. Some recent studies have found that eliminating the asterisk and making fields voluntary can actually improve conversion results because it attracts a more qualified prospect.

The website is also ideal as a fulfillment tool for lead-generation campaigns. Instead of sending out printed collateral material or white papers, invite responders to download the material from your website. This enables you to update the material regularly and to avoid the carrying costs of warehousing printed brochures. You can also make the materials customizable before download, so the prospect receives only what matters most to him or her. An added benefit is that you can track downloads and opens easily with your web analytics software.

GLAD TO SEE YOU VISITED OUR SITE!

Now a new way to capture visitor data on your company's B-to-B website visit has emerged, in the form of data matchback to the company domain name of the visitor. Plexis Healthcare Systems, a provider of insurance claim management software, uses a service called VisitorTrack for this purpose.

Here's how it works. When someone searches around the web and stops by the Plexis site, VisitorTrack grabs the IP address from the visitor's browser and identifies the visitor's company and the keywords the person was searching on. This is matched against other data about the company—for example, online data such as other visitors to the site from the same company, or offline data such as company address, industry, individual contacts, and so on. A report is generated and delivered back to Plexis for follow up.

From Plexis' point of view, knowing that people from a certain firm have been trolling around its website is valuable information. A sales call into that firm is productive.

According to J. T. Gillett, marketing manager at Plexis, the service has been a hit: "Our target for VisitorTrack is 10–15 leads per month, as determined by the number of visits, the visitors' line of business, and our ability to provide services for that line of business. VisitorTrack consistently generates 15–20 leads per month and opens many doors for our sales team. VisitorTrack has been instrumental in Plexis' invitation to submit several RFPs to a variety of prospects, including very large organizations. For us, one sale can account for between $150,000 and $2 million in revenue."

Identifying visiting companies by their IP addresses and then taking some outbound sales or marketing action into that company is still in the experimental stages. Although legal, the technique is viewed with suspicion by some marketers. Clearly, the outbound contact to the visiting company should be handled with sensitivity.

IP address identification can be done via your website analytics software or automated via an outside vendor, such as NetFactor or Demandbase.

Trade Shows with a Highly Qualified Audience

Exhibiting at trade shows and conferences is a time-honored way to get in front of customers and prospects in a focused, concentrated manner. Attendees are often highly qualified, their minds are on business at the show, and they seek solutions to business problems. Business marketers spend an average of 18.6 percent of their budgets on trade shows, according to a study from the Business Marketer Association, and most of that is targeted to sales lead generation and finding new customers.

However, trade show marketing is expensive, costing an average of $215 per contact, according to Exhibit Surveys, Inc. That's why it's important to select shows carefully and based on the likelihood of a strong concentration of potential buyers on the show floor. Broadly based, horizontal shows simply involve too much waste.

DON'T FORGET REFERRAL (VIRAL) MARKETING FOR LEAD GENERATION

From a marketer's point of view, referrals are an outstanding source of new business. Recommendations from a colleague have great credibility, so not only are referred prospects likely to be qualified, they are also likely to be motivated. The only downside of referral marketing is that you can't hope to get enough referred business to sustain your needs for growth.

Because of the Internet, "referral marketing" has morphed into "viral marketing." But it's essentially the same thing. The Internet's speed and informality lends itself well to referral practices.

Keep these points in mind when you apply referral marketing to the lead-generation process:

- Review all your marketing communications—including your content marketing materials—and add a referral request where appropriate. Consider such spots as the PS in your letters, on your home page, and as a call-out on billing statements.

- Conduct regular referral-request campaigns to your current customer base. You might want to offer an incentive to both the referrer and the referred to increase response.

- Place a pass-along request at the bottom of your emails—especially those that contain valuable information or an offer. Make the copy friendly and warm, and give a good reason why the recipient should want to help you. For example: *"Our business grows primarily through referrals from our satisfied customers. If you are happy with our work, please tell your friends and colleagues. Thank you!"*

Set the Stage for Lead Generation with PR

Building awareness is a crucial early stage in the lead-generation process. But awareness generators that are typical in consumer markets—broadcast television, for example—are out of the question for all but the broadest B-to-B categories. This is where PR comes in. In the form of media relations, analyst relations, and blogger relations, PR delivers awareness in business markets at a low cost and with high credibility. It's not easy to generate, but the tried and true techniques—contributed articles to trade publications, whitepapers, and news "manufactured" by original research—should be a part of every B-to-B prospecting program.

THE POWER OF THE TELEPHONE: STILL BUSY, RINGING UP BIG BUCKS

The telephone works as a tool by itself or in combination with other media at nearly every stage of the B-to-B sales and marketing process. Consider these applications for this highly versatile tool:

- **Market research.** Even though the Internet has become a leading medium for survey and focus group research, the phone still has its uses. It allows more reactive intelligence to be applied to the Q&A process, and, in the right hands, allows the caller to probe and gain unusual insight into customer needs and motivations.

- **Inquiry qualification.** Traditionally, the phone was the primary medium for outbound contact to assess the quality of a campaign inquiry. Email has come up quickly as a useful alternative, but a combination of the two is probably ideal.

- **Lead nurturing.** Again, a combination of the phone with other media, such as email, direct mail, events, webinars, and newsletters, can be used to keep unqualified leads warm until they are ready to see a salesperson.

- **Setting sales appointments.** This is a perfect phone use, because it's the only medium that supports the sophisticated level of interaction needed to both qualify prospects and gain their agreement to take a meeting.

- **Lead development, or high-end relationship management.** This application uses highly skilled and experienced professionals, often retired executives, to conduct top-quality conversations with senior targets.

- **Data hygiene.** The phone is perfect for calling into key accounts to confirm titles, phone numbers, buying role, and so on, and it's perfect to probe other matters to identify business opportunity.

- **"Guided voice mail" support.** Pioneered by companies like Box Pilot and VoiceLogic, this process involves a live phone call to probe around and identify the right voice mail box, and then drop in a canned voice message. The telemarketing reps also report back on what they've learned about the players and their contact information, which becomes valuable fodder for the database.

- **Live Internet chat.** When visitors to your website have questions, it's helpful to offer a call back from a live phone rep, to answer questions while the iron is hot.

- **Customer winback.** When a customer goes dormant, an inquiry by phone is an excellent way to identify the problem and perhaps prevent defection in the first place.

B-to-B Lead Generation Media: Three to Avoid

As a rule, the media discussed in the following sections should be avoided for cold prospecting. That being said, as is true with all rules, there are plenty of exceptions.

Print Advertising

Print ads can be excellent lead generators in trade and business publications. So, why are they on this list of media to avoid? For the most part, the problem is one of strategy, not medium. Most ad budgets are controlled by marketing communicators without direct-response marketing backgrounds. They let designers, instead of copywriters, drive the creative, resulting in ads that might look sensational and deliver a powerful branding message but do not contain an effective offer or call to action—essential to lead generation.

I say, "for the most part," because there is one form of print advertising in which the medium *is* the problem: Reader's Service Cards, also known as "bingo cards." These are bound-in card stock inserts filled with three-digit numbers that correspond to numbers printed on the bottom of each ad in the publication. Readers circle the numbers of the ads that interest them and send in the completed bingo card to the publisher, who passes on the readers' names as "leads" to each advertiser. The problem is that the so-called leads arrive months later and are generally worthless. You're better off creating your own targeted, measurable direct response ads for print media. This medium is generally in decline—for good reason.

That said, trade publications and certain business publications can be successful environments for lead-generation advertising if you follow the rules of direct-response communications and create the ad with response in mind. But, because there are so many more powerful media available to you, I recommend you start with them first and test your way into print later.

 Tip

Business people need information to do their jobs and are likely to frequent websites where that information is available. For that reason, well targeted banner advertising can work for lead generation. Start with the websites of the trade publications. Your agency can help with further media selection and negotiation (banner rates may be highly negotiable, and some are sold on a pay-per-click basis). Be sure to design the ad to motivate response, with an offer and a call to action.

Broadcast Advertising

In most cases, there is simply too much waste involved in TV or radio broadcasting ads to justify the expense. TV's prohibitively high costs are an additional barrier, but if you can figure out a way to zero in on an appropriate sector, radio can work. Bill Hebel, former SVP and media director at the Chicago agency Slack Barshinger (now Slack and Company), found that he could reach blue-collar targets like plumbers and electricians during early morning slots while the contractors were already out for the day in their trucks. The strategy had an additional advantage: the slots aired before the expensive "drive time" rates kicked in.

Email to Cold Prospects

Email is cheap, but the scourge of spam has made it generally undesirable as a cold prospecting medium. B-to-B marketers often find lower cost-per-inquiry results from direct mail and other media, despite the temptingly low cost of email. The reason is that an email from an unknown source is too easy to delete—if it ever gets past the layers of spam filters in its way.

On the other hand, email is a hugely important part of the lead generation, tracking, and management process as a whole. After you have persuaded someone to show interest, email is the perfect medium for staying in touch and moving the prospect along the sales cycle. Karen Breen Vogel, president and CEO of the interactive agency ClearGauge, points out that e-newsletters are particularly effective in this regard, especially in narrow niches when the content can be made highly relevant to the industry.

 Tip

Electronic newsletters, primarily seen as a relationship management tool, can also serve as a new lead-generating tool with the addition of a "viral," or pass-along message that invites readers to forward it to their friends and colleagues. Be sure to embed a subscription link, so those recipients can then subscribe easily themselves.

In summary, the best media for prospecting are:

- Outbound telemarketing
- Direct mail, including dimensional mail
- Search engine marketing
- Your website
- Trade shows (with a highly qualified audience)

The least-productive media for prospecting are:

- Print advertising

- Broadcast advertising

- Solo email

- Trade shows (horizontal shows)

Using Web 2.0 for Lead Generation

First there was the web, and then there was Web 2.0, characterized by a shift in power from web publishers to web users. Most observers agree that we are moving closer to the utopian vision for the Internet in which the network is the platform, and all involved have equal access. Blogs, podcasts, video, and social networks have worked their way into a B-to-B marketer's toolkit. This section discusses how to harness the enormous potential of Web 2.0 for lead generation.

Blogs

By some estimates, over 150 million public blogs exist in 2011, but only a small fraction of them is read in any volume. Many companies have added blogs to their websites. So should you bother? Well, you should consider it carefully. Here's why:

- Blog readers and responders serve as a source of new business contacts. Robert Lesser, president of Direct Impact Marketing, recently found that blogs received a 12 percent share among responders who named the most user-friendly and affordable tools they actively use for lead generation.

- Blog postings freshen up your website, attracting higher organic result listings on search engines.

Experts recommend taking a helpful, respectful approach—as opposed to hyping your own products—for company blogs. Here's some great advice from Ted Birkhahn of the PR firm Peppercom: "Test the waters by reading the blogs in your field, and adding non-sales-y comments to posts. Once you have a feel for the environment, then experiment with your own blog." To generate a lead, you can provide a reference to useful content and drive readers to a landing page, where you can capture their contact information and begin a relationship.

ASSESSING COST PER LEAD BY MEDIUM

Hubspot surveyed marketers on which media produced "lower than your average" cost for lead generation, show in Table 5.3. Keep in mind that Hubspot is an inbound marketing company focused on social media, so it's not surprising that their results reinforce the low cost of digital media. Also keep in mind that once an inquiry is generated, it must convert to qualified, and then to sales, so the cost per lead alone is not the whole story.

Table 5.3   Where Marketers Find the Lowest Cost Per Lead

Medium for Lead Generation	Percent of Marketers Estimating the Medium as Producing Lower Than Average Cost Per Lead
Blog/social media	55%
Email marketing	49%
SEO	48%
Direct mail	34%
SEM (pay per click advertising)	32%
Telemarketing	29%
Trade shows	18%

Micro-Blogging

Micro-blogging short (140 character) messages to "followers" has taken off and provides not only another "touch" in the communication stream, but also an effective way to identify new prospects through viral pass-along. Best practices in using Twitter, LinkedIn, and other micro-blogging platforms for lead generation include:

- Providing informative content with links pointing to a landing page where you can stimulate contact capture.

- Monitoring online discussion and respond quickly to complaints or customer feedback.

- Devoting sufficient resources to the medium to keep the conversation going.

Video

Video is blasting onto the scene with multiple applications, feeding a public weaned on electronic games, infatuated with YouTube, and increasingly impatient with static forms of communication. When CMP Media launched a daily video broadcast to tech buyers on TechWeb, its ad spots sold like hotcakes. According to David Azulay, vice president of client services at The Kern Organization, adding a video introduction to your company website's landing page is a key to success. "Enthusiasm for video is at an all-time high," notes Azulay. "We are finding that a credible spokesperson giving a short video introduction to the product or service can increase conversions and downloads by 20–50 percent." Video can be used for multiple purposes, and is particularly well suited to product demonstration and customer testimonials.

Webinars

Web-based seminars, also known as "webinars" or "webcasts," have come into wide use in B-to-B, usually later in the sales cycle when buyers determine their specifications and which vendors to use. But they can also work early in the sales cycle, when the prospect is not even aware of a problem.

Webinars work best when you have a lot of information to communicate, especially when your product or service can solve a pressing business problem faced by customers. It also helps when you have a hot topic, a strong offer, and a highly targeted group of prospects.

RSA Security, a Bedford MA provider of enterprise security software, used a webinar to help launch a new product that supports "federated identity," meaning the capability for companies to share sensitive employee identity information. The webinar was targeted to IT professionals who have an interest in security issues. A leading industry analyst was the featured presenter, and email invitations were sent to over 100,000 contacts from RSA Security's inquiry database and from websites specializing in security topics. The invitation was sweetened with an offer to win a set of Bose noise-canceling headphones in a drawing among webinar attendees.

How did it work? Michael Veit, manager of direct marketing at RSA Security, set his goal for the event at 1,000 registrations, 400 attendees, and 200 qualified sales leads. He ended up with 1,132 registrations, 481 attendees, and 233 qualified leads. Even better, the conversion rate on registrants was 2.2 percent.

Podcasts

Delivering snippets of downloadable audio, podcasts are taking their place alongside email, telephone, PDF downloads, and the myriad of other touch options that B-to-B marketers use to migrate customers and prospects along the long sales cycle.

The predominant use of podcasts among business marketers is to deliver product information or establish "thought leadership," with a short discussion or interview on a business problem of interest. But beware: The podcast is a passive medium, dependent on users' motivation to visit your site and go to the trouble of downloading the audio material. That means you'll need to factor in the additional expense to promote the podcast itself. On the plus side, podcasts are inexpensive to produce.

In summary, a podcast is not a tool for generating cold inquiries—except by viral pass-along—but is excellent for lead nurturing and relationship marketing throughout the business-buying process.

Syndication

Syndicated media, like RSS, allows fresh content to be streamed to subscribers as it is produced, and has been a productive direct-marketing medium. After you invest in signing up subscribers—whether through your website or through social media—you have a new, automated and low-cost channel for staying in touch and keeping current. RSS is also said to be a useful way to get information out in a world where corporate spam filters block so much email.

But the RSS adoption curve has been slower than some of the other Web 2.0 media, and some observers think it's on the way out. A KnowledgeStorm Universal McCann study found that among tech buyers—whom you would expect to be early adopters—only 31 percent said they subscribe or use RSS readers. This compares with 80 percent who said they read blogs. RSS may very likely fade away—or be replaced by other emerging media over time.

Social Networks

Sizable social networks for business people have sprung up, including LinkedIn and Facebook, and marketers are out there experimenting avidly with them. Among the applications showing promise for lead generation are:

- **Cooperative list development.** LinkedIn encourages individual business people to leverage the network to connect with others who have connections with particular companies or lines of business. LinkedIn allows banner advertising and paid email to reach prospects. Companies like Jigsaw and Spoke combine social networking with cooperative list development, allowing sales people to contribute and to collect contact information on sales targets.

- **Referrals.** Social networks take word-of-mouth marketing to the next level. Asking a current customer for a referral is the lowest cost source of new customers you can get.

- **Advertising.** LinkedIn and Facebook provide plenty of banner advertising options. Combining a strong offer and call to action with an effective landing page can deliver plenty of valuable inquiries. Targeting and segmentation is still fairly rudimentary on social networks, so they may be most effective with broadly focused products and services.

- **Contests and promotions.** Social networkers—even serious business people—respond to contests and promos online, and they are also likely to pass the deal along to their colleagues virally. So many marketers find that classic promotions work well in this environment for stimulating responses and building databases. Just be sure you use an experienced agency to help keep you out of trouble, because promotions and sweepstakes are so highly regulated.

- **Market research.** Communispace creates web-based communities of customers and prospects for companies like HP and CDW, using a combination of social networking and good old-fashioned consumer panel techniques that enable marketers to get deep customer insight and feedback about products, services, and the works.

 Tip

There are some exciting potential prospecting tools for business marketers on the horizon. For example, Media Director Bill Hebel has found gold in online contextual advertising. Text links, especially, are viewed as editorial, so they can be attractive when served up on a keyword-specific basis. "People are ignoring banners these days," says Hebel. "Contextual ads are not only more relevant; the CPMs are cheaper, too."

How to Select the Right Media Mix

Selecting the exact media mix to meet the lead flow requirements of sales will be an iterative process. First, establish with the sales team their monthly (or weekly, or quarterly) requirements for the number of qualified leads per rep (or by product, territory, or whatever is needed). Then, plan carefully the media mix that will feed the machine.

The media mix is a function of several variables, which you need to research:

- The ROI each medium can deliver.

- The medium's availability. For example, when are the industry trade shows scheduled throughout the year? Profitable banner ad media might exist, but can you get enough of them to satisfy your needs for leads?

- The campaign's time horizon. Electronic media are faster to create than direct mail, for example.

- The lead flow requirements. For example, sales might need more leads in the first and fourth quarters.

Use a spreadsheet as an iterative planning tool. Lay out the media options on your spreadsheet and start tweaking. Table 5.4 presents a simple example of how this can work. (Please note: These numbers are hypothetical and not intended necessarily to represent current average costs or response rates.)

Table 5.4   Calculating Cost Per Lead by Medium

Medium	Volume	Cost	Response Rate	Gross Inquiries	Qualification Rate	Qualified Leads	Cost/Lead
Mail	30M	$1500/M	2%	600	25%	150	$300
Print	40M	$100/M	.5%	200	20%	40	$100
Trade show	—	$15,000/event	—	400	10%	40	$375
Banner ad	5M	$50/M	.5%	25	40%	10	$25
SEM	—	$1/click	—	100	10%	10	$10

You can expand this spreadsheet to include other key variables, such as timing and geographic territory requirements. Notice that this spreadsheet breaks out the expected qualification rate by inquiry source, a refinement that can assist in your making the best media mix decisions.

You are likely to end up with some inexpensive leads in your mix. The unfortunate thing is that, typically, these leads are not enough to meet your growth needs or support your sales force's quota. So you'll need to select several options, ranking them by ROI, availability, and your lead flow criteria to come up with the optimal mix.

Mixing It Up: Multiple Media

Business marketers know that when it comes to selecting media, the whole is greater than the sum of its parts. Multiple media can work beautifully together, delivering a better response and lower cost per lead than each element working on its own. Here are some combos that deliver:

- **Mail and phone.** This tried-and-true, one-two punch combines the deep penetration of the telephone with the persuasive power of the mail. Just make sure the follow-up call is a substantive part of moving the prospect along the buying process and not simply an empty confirmation that the mailing piece arrived. Note: Some telemarketing experts recommend that you avoid mentioning the mail piece during the phone call, because it diverts the discussion from the objective at hand, which is to generate a lead.

- **Phone and mail.** Some businesses switch the order of the previous, telephoning first and following up with mail. This approach works well when asking for a specific action, such as attendance at a seminar. Calling is also a good way to qualify inquirers from trade shows, where many people may browse at your booth but only a portion of them will ever become qualified buyers. Use a phone call to screen out the duds rather than waste money on an expensive fulfillment package.

- **Email and mail or other media.** As long as you already have some kind of business relationship with the target, email enhances the communications mix due to its low cost. It's not a good choice for cold prospecting because so much of it will be spammed out, but for inquirers and current customers, it combines nicely with other communications to reinforce key messages and provide an additional touch.

- **Postcards and other types of mail or other media.** Some marketers find that varying the mail format is helpful. Begin with a series of postcards, and follow up with a letter and a phone call or email. Because the phone is so powerful and intrusive, you may find that a simple postcard in advance is enough to grab attention.

- **Print ads and mail.** Redeploy print ads by sending reprints accompanied by a letter saying, "In case you missed our recent ad in such-and-such a magazine...." This technique can provide a good excuse to contact your customers and inquirers directly.

- **Awareness campaigns and other media.** Mass media awareness campaigns, in such channels as television and print, provide excellent support for a lead-generation program. If you can time your campaigns to coincide with or follow shortly after a branding campaign, your response rates will be stronger than usual.

Integrated Marketing

Multiple media working together generate better results than single media, with one big proviso: The messages must be consistent across media. An inconsistent message can cause confusion and erode the value of the brand.

Pulling this off is not always easy, especially in medium-to-large companies. You have to coordinate functional silos with their own managers, vocabularies, cultures, budgets, and objectives. This requires tenacity, a focus on the customer experience, and support from senior management. But the payoff is colossal. All outbound contacts with customers, whether they are customer service messages or even billing-related messages, can potentially be harnessed for the lead effort.

The simplest way to gain this kind of leverage is to put the company website URL, which should have a registration offer prominently placed on the home page, on all messages received by the customer. The same principle applies to customer touch points that are less obviously part of marketing communications, such as packaging, point of purchase displays, billing statements—any point where the customer comes in contact with the product or service.

Similarly, with a little effort, some marketing communications can do even more to support lead generation. To stimulate your thinking:

- Include a white paper offer, with response instructions such as an 800 number or a web response URL, in every press release.

- Ensure that all brand-awareness advertising includes an offer, a call to action, and a response device.

- When executives give speeches, invite your customers and prospects to attend.

- Include a special offer in your press releases. If the journalist finds it of interest and includes mention of the offer in the story, you are likely to receive some response.

WHAT'S THE HANGUP WITH VOICE MAIL?

Voice mail has become a big part of the B-to-B marketing toolkit and deserves your strategic consideration. Upward of 85 percent of outbound business calls go to voice mail. You don't want to waste that touch. But what kind of voice mail message should you leave?

Mike Chaplo, a long-time sales executive, speaks for many in the industry when he says firmly, "Don't leave one. Hang up. Call back again, and keep trying. If after five or six attempts you still can't get through, send an email that asks what the best time is to call. Your objective in business is to have a conversation, not to leave an annoying message."

Other marketers see the situation as a huge opportunity. According to Rob Lail, founder and president of MarketMakers, a B-to-B teleservices firm in the Philadelphia area, voice mail has a powerful role to play in a campaign—if you plan for it. "The most important thing is to prepare a superb script," says Lail. "It has to be professional, but not sound canned. We provide our reps with scripts, but they only use them as a guide. They need to know the material cold, and speak to it naturally, so they sound confident."

Lail says the single most effective use of voice mail is in event marketing, for extending an invitation or reminding prospects to attend a seminar, conference, webcast or some other live appointment. "Reminder calls to seminar attendees who have agreed to come can improve their actual attendance by 40 percent," says Lail.

John Hasbrouck, president and CEO of NewLeads, a provider of trade show contact follow-up services, recommends the following path for your voice mail message to garner maximum attention and response:

- **Pain.** Start with their problem. Don't start with yourself.

- **Hope.** State your offering. For example, "We solve that problem."

- **References.** Name a few customers who will be familiar and credible.

- **Features.** If you can squeeze in one or two supporting features, do so. But keep the total to 30 seconds.

- **Response.** Tell them what to do and how. For example, "If you want to know more, please give me a call."

For a convenient summary of the media types discussed in this chapter, see Table 5.5. Keep in mind that new media come along regularly, so be prepared to expand the list as time goes on.

Table 5.5   Outbound Lead Generation Campaign Media Types

Medium	Strengths	Weaknesses	Best Applications
Banner advertising	Fast turnaround and results Deals available	Limited workable outlets Small creative space	Inquiry generation Brand awareness
Blogs	Inexpensive Influential, if done well	Requires persistence and resources	Brand awareness Lead nurturing
Catalogs	Inexpensive (versus field sales) Valued by customers as a reference	Expensive (versus e-commerce) Prone to obsolescence	Retention Sales
Email	Fast turnaround and results Inexpensive	Permission required Limited creative options Limited address availability	Lead qualification Lead nurturing Retention
Mail	Many formats available Highly flexible to support the need Wide variety of lists available	Expensive per piece Long planning cycle	Inquiry generation Response handling Lead nurturing Retention
Micro-blogging	Low cost Targeted audience	Limited creative space Expense to build a following	Inquiry generation Lead nurturing Retention
Mobile	Low cost Targeted audience	Requires permission	Lead qualification Lead nurturing

continued

Table 5.5   Outbound Lead Generation Campaign Media Types (continued)

Medium	Strengths	Weaknesses	Best Applications
Newsletters (email)	Inexpensive High pass-along propensity	Difficult to sustain editorial quality	Inquiry generation Retention
Newsletters (print)	Inexpensive High perceived value	Difficult to sustain editorial quality	Lead nurturing Retention
Podcasts	Inexpensive Targeted audience	Expense to build a subscriber base	Lead nurturing Retention
PR	Inexpensive for building brand awareness	Difficult to manage or predict results Not designed for response generation	Awareness
Print advertising	Broad reach Efficient	Less targeted Print budgets often controlled by brand marketers	Inquiry generation Brand awareness
RSS feeds	Avoids spam filters Interested audience	Shallow penetration	Inquiry generation Retention
Social networks	Low cost	Difficult to predict or control	Inquiry generation Retention
SEM/SEO	Attracts prospects in-market Global reach Controllable costs	Limited universe	Inquiry generation

continued

Table 5.5   Outbound Lead Generation Campaign Media Types (continued)

Medium	Strengths	Weaknesses	Best Applications
Seminars	Conveys deep product information Develops personal relationships	Inefficient Limited reach	Lead nurturing Retention
Telephone	Intrusive Flexible Universally available	Recipient is often unreachable Expensive	Response handling Lead qualification Lead nurturing
Trade shows	Qualified reach	Limited reach Expensive	Inquiry generation Brand awareness
Video	High appeal Vivid product demonstration	Increases banner expense	Inquiry generation Lead nurturing Retention
Webinars	Broad reach Inexpensive/M	Imperfect technology	Lead nurturing Retention
Website	Easy to update Multipurpose applicability Holds deep product information	Passive, non-intrusive	Brand awareness Inquiry generation Response handling Retention

6

Campaign Execution

Prospecting is hard work. You want to find the maximum number of likely targets, reach them through the most efficient media, motivate them to raise their hands, and achieve the lowest possible cost per inquiry—all while maintaining the quality level of inquiries that will convert to qualified leads and eventually convert to a sale. This is a tall order, and it begins with identifying the most likely targets for your campaign.

Campaign Target Selection: Finding the Winning Combination

Most business-to-business (B-to-B) direct marketers use a combination of approaches to selecting campaign targets. These include:

- **Current customers.** If you introduce a new product or service, your best prospects are going to be current customers. They already have a relationship with you. You know how to reach them. This is heaven when it comes to prospecting. Consider the variety of ways to look at current customers, and select among them based on your campaign's strategic objectives:

  - Current buyers at current sites

  - Additional prospective buyers at current sites

  - Similar titles at new sites within current enterprises

- **Look-alike prospects.** Profile your top customers and identify similar business people based on characteristics such as industry, company size, title, and job function. Database firms such as InfoGroup and D&B can help you build profiles and compare them against large databases to find the closest matches.

- **Affinity groups.** Audience selection is based on affinities such as industry vertical and title. Product interest is the next step. This leads to affinity-driven media such as product category buyer lists, publication subscriber lists, and functional websites that serve segments such as engineers or HR managers.

So it's a good idea to review these three approaches and develop your campaign targeting strategy with a judicious combination of targets from current customer segments, prospects from the greater universe who have similar characteristics to your top customers, and prospects selected by criteria such as title, job function, company size, and industry. But there are many segmentation variables to consider in B-to-B lead-generation campaigning. Let's look at the list of possibilities.

B-to-B Segmentation Variables

When developing campaign targeting strategies, consider the segmentation variables typical of B-to-B markets. These are:

- The relationship existing today between the company and the buyer (prospect, first-time buyer, core customer, and defector)

- Geographics (country, region, state, and ZIP code)
- Demographics (job function, buying role, title, age, and so on)
- "Firmographics" (company size, industry, and purchasing behavior)
- Purchase history (product purchase history, revenue, and lifetime value)

Pick the Perfect Platform

Once you've decided on campaign targets, it's time to consider the messaging strategies that will motivate them to raise their hands and express interest in your product or service. Message platforms encapsulate the benefits that you believe will appeal most strongly to your prospective audience. Developing the right message platform should be relatively easy if your pre-campaign research has done its job in identifying the needs, the preferences, and the interests of your target audience.

The next step is to convert the features of your product or service into benefits, and then select the benefits that are most meaningful to your prospects. The benefits can be personal, business-oriented, or both.

Converting features into benefits is an essential part of campaign message development. The best way to go at this is to make a list of the key features of the product and translate each one into a benefit that is meaningful to the customer. Put yourself in the mind of the target audience, and ask yourself, "What's in it for me? Why should I care?"

For example, say one of the great features of your product is that you support it with excellent customer service. A feature statement in such a situation might be, "Our service center is staffed around the clock by highly skilled specialists." But, when you convert that feature into a benefit meaningful to the prospect, it might emerge as: "You'll rest easy knowing that help is available 24/7 to help you solve any problems."

Some sample message platforms in B-to-B include:

- **Save time.** Variations on this message might be: "Get to market quicker" or "Reduce manufacturing overhead."
- **Save money.** This can be recast into other profit-oriented formats, such as, "Sell more" or "Spend less."
- **Grow your business.** "Penetrate new markets." "Find new customers. Sell them more."
- **Make your job more secure.** As in the old adage: "No one ever got fired for buying IBM."

- **Increase efficiency or productivity.** "Do more with less."

- **Make more money.** "Increase sales." "Increase profits."

- **Avoid stress or hardship.** "Take the strain off your shoulders."

- **Dispel fear of the unknown, or loss, or failure.** "Guaranteed results."

- **Make your job easier.** "Simplify fulfillment."

Don't ignore one of the most powerful benefits you can stress in lead generation: *the offer itself*. In fact, marketers have found that a message platform that focuses directly on "selling the offer" can be the most powerful way to deliver on campaign objectives. Why? Because the purpose of a lead-generation message is to stimulate an immediate response, to motivate the target to say, "Yes, I want that!" The offer itself is the incentive that triggers the action. So, rather than selling the product or service, and focusing on their key benefits, making the offer the hero of the campaign message can be the more powerful approach.

 Tip

Enlist the help of the sales force in developing message platforms. Their daily interactions with customers and prospects give them the inside scoop about what's on the mind of your targets.

Reaching the Consumer Inside

The secret to successful lead generation creative is to understand the customer's needs, attitudes, and motivations. A bigger secret is that inside every business buyer is a human being with personal needs, fears, and aspirations. Although business buyers need facts and persuasive arguments to justify a purchase to their company—whose money they're spending—they also respond to emotional appeals. They represent their company, but they have needs, fears, and aspirations all their own. So developing powerful message platforms, compelling copy, and eye-catching art in lead generation requires a deep understanding of the business buyer both as a consumer and as a company representative.

Here's an example that comes from the leading B-to-B copywriter, Bob Bly. Bly was asked by a seminar organizer to help market a seminar called "Interpersonal Skills for IT Professionals." The first thing Bly did was analyze the beliefs, feelings, and desires of information technology workers, to develop an understanding of what was going on in their minds. He concluded that they generally believed that they were smarter than others in the company, that these people felt frustrated about a lot of things, and that they desired nothing more than to be left alone to do their work. Based on these insights, Bly crafted a new headline for the seminar, which really resonated with this audience: "Inside: Important Information for Any IT Professional Who Wanted to Say to an End-User: 'Go to Hell!'"

 Tip

> Messages that tend to appeal to IT buyers focus on how the product is easy to install with no downtime, so that end-users won't complain. The best messages to line-of-business buyers focus on how the product is easy to use, saves you time and money, and helps you get your job done.

You can organize your multi-touch campaigns for maximal effectiveness by combining your analysis of your prospect's buying process (see Chapter 2, "Campaign Planning") and the most appropriate campaign media (see Chapter 5, "Campaign Media Selection") with the target individuals' buying roles. As an example, look at Table 6.1, where the individual contact's buying role is combined with the individual's buying process stage, and possible media options are identified for each combination. Earlier in the buying process, you need to use more intrusive media, such as direct mail or telephone, to get the audience's attention and kick off a relationship. As the prospects are are researching solutions, you want to establish yourself as a thought leader and a trusted resource. Later, when they know you, and you are actively involved in solving their business problems, communications media designed to educate and move the relationship forward are the most productive.

Table 6.1 Mapping Campaign Touches to Buying Role and Process

Buying Role	Identify Need	Research	Short List	Negotiate
Decision maker	Dimensional mail	Research report posted at website	Email	Face-to-face sales
Specifier	Letter mail	White paper delivered via Twitter or a technical community, such as IT Toolbox	Webinar/road show	
Influencer	Post card, business Q&A site such as Focus or Quora	White paper delivered on a blog or via Twitter	Webinar/road show	
User	Letter mail	Case study delivered on a blog or via Twitter or LinkedIn	Blog	
Purchasing			Letter mail, email	Inside sales

HOW TO CONVERT YOUR PRODUCT FEATURES INTO CUSTOMER BENEFITS

Business marketers frequently fall into the trap of stressing product features in their communications. This is especially true in technical fields, where product managers tend to get excited about all the wonderful elements they have engineered into their products.

What business marketers need to do is convert those product features into customer benefits. Marketers must understand what is on the target customer's mind, and then translate those wonderful features into benefits that are meaningful, relevant, and valuable to the customer.

One term for this approach is WIIFM, or, What's In It For Me? This is what customers care about. They care about themselves, not the product. They care about the product only insofar as it helps them. So this is what the marketer has to identify, highlight, and then communicate.

But don't take this to mean that you should ignore the features. Product details and specifications are needed to justify the purchase. Keep them in there—right along with the benefits.

Notice that benefits can be personal, expressed in human terms. They are often about human fears and desires. Some marketers say that the most successful products are positioned to meet one or more of the two strongest human emotions: fear and greed.

Here's an example of how product features can be recast as business or personal benefits:

Feature	Benefit
Light weight	Reduces stress; eliminates need for frequent replacement
24-hour tech support	Eliminates downtime and data loss
Multi-platform file sharing	Saves time; increases reliability
Plug and play	No connection headaches; get started immediately
Peel-off adhesive backing	Makes work-flow organization easy

Seven Steps to Successful Lead-Generation Creative

Keep these seven guidelines in mind during the lead generation campaign creative process, as you are developing the copy and design of your communications:

1. **Do your homework.** Analyze the market situation, the competitive situation, and your product's strengths and weaknesses. Research your

prospects' needs and preferences. Develop a solid value proposition and message platform.

2. **Focus on facts.** Business people need facts, so be sure to give them plenty. Motivate the product manager to spend quality time with the copywriter and art director, giving them a thorough understanding of the product and its benefits.

3. **Encourage creativity.** You need the breakthrough ideas that cut through the clutter, grab the attention of the prospect, and communicate the benefits of your product or service. Balance facts with creativity and features with benefits.

4. **Aim for response only.** You don't have to tell a prospect everything about your product in each communication. All you need is enough to elicit a response and move the process along.

5. **Make an offer.** You need an offer, presented in a compelling way, to get a response. You need to make clear what you want the prospect to do, and make it easy to respond.

6. **Integrate marketing communications.** Integrate your direct response communications strategy with your brand communications. For instance, as you ask for a response, be sure the message reflects the look and feel of the rest of the communications mix. Your lead generation will support your brand messaging and will gain leverage from whatever awareness has already been built.

7. **Use experienced professionals.** Use a copywriter and art director with a strong B-to-B direct-response background for maximum results.

Copy Tips: What Sells

B-to-B direct response communications call for a special kind of copywriting compared to general advertising copy. Inspect your copy against these guidelines to improve response rates:

- **Clarity.** No matter how complex the product or the industry or how well schooled you consider your customer, keep the writing simple. Make sure your offer can be grasped immediately. Avoid marketing jargon such as "leading provider" and "synergy."

- **Benefits.** People don't buy based on what the product does, but what it does *for them*. Convert your product features into benefits that are meaningful to your target audience.

- **Concrete information.** Describe your product's benefits specifically. Don't just say, "It saves money." Specify how and how much.

- **Power words.** Some words suffer from being tired, overused, or vague. So look for more dynamic, specific alternatives. For example, substitute "industry specialist" for "salesperson." Or, offer a "free, no-obligation consultation" instead of a "sales call."

- **Guarantees.** Use testimonials and success stories. Stress your company's stability and long track record in the industry. Make customers feel comfortable; they need to know that doing business with you won't jeopardize their job security.

- **The basics:** Use clear, friendly, personal writing. Provide several ways to respond. Remember, you are talking to an individual person, so make good use of emotional triggers in your copy.

ATTENTION-GETTING WORDS

Successful direct-response copywriters have learned over the years to incorporate words like these to grab attention and motivate action:

Advice	Proven
Announcing	Revolutionary
At last	Save
Because	Secrets
Confidential	Smart
Congratulations	Special invitation
Free	Success
Guaranteed	Wanted
How to	Which
Introducing	Who else
Limited-time	Why
New	Yes
Now	

Design Tips: What Works

This may cause offense among graphic designers, but the truth is that copy trumps art when it comes to driving response in B-to-B markets. The reason is that copywriting is where the persuasion—the selling—takes place. The role of the design is to deliver the copy and the offer with clarity and interest. Design should not call attention to itself. Above all, the design should not get in the way. Keep in mind these tips as you review your lead-generation design options:

- **Accessibility.** Graphic design is not just about photos and illustrations. It's also about accessibility and navigation. Design should help organize the copy and draw in readers, moving them along toward the call to action.

- **Well used space.** Take the physical space you need to deliver the message in a compelling way, but no more. The message should drive the size and format of your communication versus the other way around.

- **Testing into new formats.** Start with the standards and test the rest. For example, if using direct mail, begin with the proven direct-response elements: an outer envelope, letter, response device, and brochure. Test against these elements in other formats, such as self-mailers and postcards. In banner advertising, begin with a simple headline and call to action. Then test your way into animation or drop-down boxes.

- **Business letters.** No matter the medium, strive to include a true business letter in the communication. Nothing is more powerful than a personal message, from one individual to another, whether in postal mail, email, on a landing page, or inside a brochure. Make sure it's signed by a real person.

- **Pass-alongs.** Include a pass-along request at appropriate points in your communications. If in the mail, for example, ideal spots are the postscript, the order form, or behind the window where the pass-along message is visible when the envelope contents are removed. In an email, use the P.S. This increases your reach to additional prospects at a low cost.

- **Repetition.** Repeat the offer and the response media options (phone, email address, URL, and fax) on the response device, whether a business reply card or a landing page.

- **Option to defer.** Add a deferral option to every response device. For example, "Not interested now. Please contact me again in ____ months." You increase response and gain leads to put into the pipeline for later conversion.

CREATIVE CHECKLIST FOR HEADLINES

These time-tested strategic creative approaches serve as a powerful basis for message development—either in the headline or as a copy opener:

- **News.** "Here's a way to increase your sales, fast."

- **Emotional connection.** "Doesn't it drive you crazy when a customer service rep puts you on hold?"

- **Problem/solution.** "Is your factory floor covered with dangerous greasy film? We can help."

- **Testimonial.** "Just listen to what our satisfied customers say about us."

- **Compelling question.** "Would you like to sell more and spend less in the very next quarter?"

- **Guarantee.** "Sixty-day free trial, and your money back if you are not completely satisfied."

- **Benefit.** "Here's an idea that you can put to use tomorrow."

- **Fear.** "What would you do if you lost your job tomorrow?"

- **Greed.** "I want to give you this special free gift just for reviewing my helpful new guide to human resource management."

How to Develop Offers They Can't Refuse

Direct-response marketing efforts all have one goal and one goal only: to trigger a response on the part of the target. It is the offer that motivates the audience to overcome their inertia and take the action you are looking for.

Your offer *must* provide a compelling reason to respond. The offer can be an incentive with personal benefit to the recipient, or it can be related to solving a business problem. Whatever incentive is selected, the offer is a critical factor in moving the prospect to action.

Here are some dos and don'ts of developing high-octane offers:

Do...

- **Keep the offer simple.** Business buying can be a long process, so it is tempting to skip to the end in one communication. Always remember that lead generation is simply about getting a response and moving the process forward one step at a time.

- **Match the offer to the customer's stage in the buying process.** If the customer needs to see a demo of the product before he or she will buy, then offer a free demonstration. See Table 6.2 for additional examples.

Table 6.2   Matching Offer to Buying Process Stage

Customer's Buying Process Stage	Media Channels	Offer Options
Identify need	Advertising, PR	Free information
Research solutions	Advertising, PR	Free premium, free trail
Develop short list	Direct mail, email, website	Free premium, trial, sample
Request proposals	Face-to-face sales	Seminar, demonstration, sales call
Review proposals	Face-to-face sales, direct mail	Trial, sample, demonstration
Negotiate	Face-to-face sales	Lunch, golf game
Select vendor	Face-to-face sales	Lunch, event tickets
Install and use	Support personnel	Consultation
Upgrade	Telesales, direct mail	Information, premium, extended warranty

- **Craft offers with perceived value.** Industry white papers are a good example of offers business buyers find worthwhile. Information that helps people do their jobs makes a fail-safe basis for offer development.

- **Try service-oriented offers.** Use faster service or higher service levels as an incentive to respond or buy.

- **Think about offers as "soft" or "hard."** Soft offers are attractive and low-risk, and they have a high perceived value and broad appeal. Free premiums such as a t-shirt or a calculator are popular soft offers in business marketing. Hard offers tend to stress business value, and they require more effort on the part of the respondent, such as attendance at a free seminar or an invitation for a sales person to call. To help you think about how hard offers and soft offers can best be applied, consider the following principles:

  - **Use a harder offer if you are looking for a more qualified prospect.** You will receive fewer responses, but there will be more likelihood to buy. This approach makes sense when you are targeting a relatively unqualified universe of prospects, and you want to attract only the wheat and leave the chaff.

  - **Use a softer offer if you are trying to increase your prospect list or widen your net.** Soft offers yield many inquiries that can be nurtured later. This is an especially useful strategy if you have a limited universe of prospects and you want to penetrate the universe as deeply as possible.

- **Use a hard offer toward the end of the buying process when the prospect is reviewing vendors and about to make a commitment.** Retention offers, such as frequency discounts, make sense after the transaction is complete.

- **Combine hard and soft offers.** Get the best of both worlds by combining the qualifying power of a hard offer with the attraction of a soft offer. As an example, you might offer a free premium (soft) in exchange for a meeting between a customer and a salesperson (hard), and explain that the salesperson will deliver the free premium on arrival.

- **Make sure the offer is clear, understandable, and compellingly stated.** The way your offer is presented—in both copy and design—impacts its effectiveness.

- **Test offers regularly.** Your testing criteria must evaluate both the front end (the initial response) and the back end (the conversion to sales). You might find that soft offers convert as well as hard ones, enabling you to increase your results and lower your marketing costs.

- **Match the offer to the medium.** What works in email or print might not work in the mail or over the phone. In search engine marketing ads, you are limited to just a few words of copy, so the offer must be simple and easy to communicate.

- **Calculate the entire cost of making the offer.** Include the costs of purchasing, fulfillment, packing, and shipping for a physical item. Information-based offers can be distributed with zero variable expense, which makes them all the more efficient.

- **Experiment with several offers in a single message.** The customer can then select the offer most appropriate to his or her stage in the buying process, whether it is a white paper, a seminar, or a sales call.

- **Keep the offer appropriate to your industry and your company image.** It goes without saying that you should avoid anything in poor taste. But the offer you choose does say something about your firm and its image. Some companies strive to associate themselves with certain levels of dignity or traditionalism, in which case they might select a polo shirt over a t-shirt as a premium. Start-up companies, on the other hand, often want to associate themselves with the latest cool tech gadget when choosing a premium offer.

Don't...

- **Don't be afraid to offer a personal benefit.** Remember the dual nature of the business buyer, who is both the company representative and the person whose response motivators are as much about his or her own benefit as the company's.

- **Don't forget basics from consumer direct marketing.** Use guarantees, stress exclusivity, make the offer easy to understand, add urgency, and always test.

- **Avoid *very* soft offers, such as sweepstakes.** These can be productive for building a database or when there are other good reasons to widen the net. But for B-to-B lead generation, this type of offer must be used with caution. If you do use a sweepstakes offer, engage a company or agency that specializes in them, so that you are in compliance with all the rules.

- **Don't listen to colleagues who argue that you don't need an offer because "the product will sell itself."** They're wrong! Use an incentive offer in *every* lead-generation communication. Without an offer, your response rate will plummet.

- **Don't ignore industry research on offer performance.** The Direct Marketing Association (DMA) publishes data about what's working across the field of consumer and B-to-B direct marketing, so it's a good idea to access that research as part of your thinking process about offer development. In Table 6.3, for example, you can see how B-to-B marketers evaluated the relative effectiveness of various offers on a scale of 1 to 5.

Table 6.3   B-to-B Incentive Offers Rated by Effectiveness

Type of Incentive Offer	Rating
Free gifts	3.43
Free information	3.64
Free/reduced shipping	2.20
Free sample	3.00
Free trial	3.13
Sweepstakes	2.83
Discounts	3.33
Buy one, get one free	2.00
Frequent buyer/loyalty program	2.20

Source: The DMA, *Getting Creative*, 2007

Types of Offers: Consider the Possibilities

When it comes to considering among the wide variety of offers available, don't hold back. Experiment with as many types of offers as you can to come up with to find the ones that bring the desired response at each stage of the buying process. The following types of offers are frequently used for lead generation and have proven their value over time:

- Free information (brochure, newsletter, white paper, case study, article reprint, video, and demo CD)

- Premium (gift, book)

- Free trial

- Free sample

- Self-assessment tool

- Seminar or webinar

- Demonstration

- Discount

- Sales call

- Free consultation or audit

- Free estimate

- Free installation

- ROI calculator

- Extended warranty

Matching Your Offer to Your Customers' Buying Processes

Just as the buying process dictates the most productive selling process, it also provides valuable guidance in selecting the most productive direct-response offer for each stage. In Table 6.2, follow the buying process down the first column. Look at the middle column for ideas about the most appropriate media channel at each stage of the process and look at the last column for possible appropriate offers. These are just examples. You would do well to lay out your target customer segment's buying process; then, experiment with your own offer development ideas at each stage.

Information, Please!

Hands down, in most B-to-B situations, an offer of some kind of information about how to do your job better, how to solve a business problem, how to save time and money, and so on drives the best results for lead generation. Why? For the same reason that "free trial" is probably the best all-around offer in consumer direct-response marketing. An offer of information combines the three magic ingredients:

- Strong appeal with high perceived value

- An innate ability to qualify the prospect

- Relatively low cost and risk

It attracts, it qualifies, and it doesn't break the bank. Bingo! The perfect offer.

Why does information pull so well? The answer can be found in the dual nature of the business buyer: equal parts company representative and consumer. The buyer is thinking both about the company and the job and his or her own personal benefit.

Information has benefits to fill the bill perfectly. These benefits are:

- Ideas for cutting costs or improving productivity

- Proof points such as testimonials, research reports, and case studies

- Insight into what's working for the competition

- Data that helps sell the idea internally

- Fresh content that makes the buyer look good, seem smart, and feel like a valued contributor to the firm

The most attractive information is specific, gives immediate assistance on the job, and is deeply relevant to the business buyer. Thus, in turn, only business people who actually have that need are likely to respond. These are innately qualified prospects. (Compare the attractiveness of an offer for "10 Tips for Making Your Business More Profitable" to an offer like a free t-shirt.)

The best thing about this kind of offer in an electronic age is the cost: next to nothing. You have to pay to acquire the piece or have it written, but when converted to a PDF downloadable from your website, the incremental cost per piece is zero. Even when packaged as a book, a CD, or a video, information is cheap on a cost/benefit basis. The variable production cost is similar to that t-shirt, but the perceived value on the part of the prospect is far higher.

Of course, "information" is not just an offer. It's a category. Information offers come in all kinds of forms, and each has its strengths and weaknesses:

- **White paper.** White papers have been somewhat abused lately, with some companies applying the term to materials that are actually glorified sales brochures. A true white paper is an objective, authoritative document on a significant topic, and true white papers are at the top of the list of strong information offers. The secret to an effective white paper today is value. Make it specific, both in title and content. Give customers an objectively written, nonsales-like piece of research that analyzes a business problem and its potential solutions. (If you do include information about your product or service, put it in a discreet sidebar.)

- **"Ten Tips" brochure.** The tips don't need to number ten exactly, but the content needs to be short, snappy, and easy to skim. See Figure 6.1 for an excellent example of this. Choose a theme that addresses an important pain point and provides real business value. Here are some examples of titles that can work:

  - Ten Tips for Making Your Business More Profitable

  - Seven Ways to Reduce Your Accounting Expenses

  - The Top Five Strategies for Cutting Cycle Time

- **Case study.** Business buyers crave case studies because they make the solution real. A case not only conveys credibility (the product works!) but also offers an appealingly voyeuristic view of *how* it works. Video case studies are even more tangible than the written word.

- **Newsletter.** Hard-copy or electronic newsletters make a powerful offer if they are clearly positioned as material that helps readers do their jobs better. The key benefit of newsletters to marketers is their use as an ongoing communication device. If the content is useful, the newsletter is a low-cost way to nurture the customer relationship over time. But self-serving copy is the kiss of death.

The best way to choose among these many types of information offers is to map the information to the prospect's stage in the buying process. For example, early in the process the buyer analyzes the business problem and researches solutions. At this stage, white papers and research reports are ideal for establishing your credibility as a supplier. Later in the process, the buyer might be interested in case studies that provide real-life examples of your product at work. Similarly, a product demo might be the perfect offer to move the prospect along the buying process.

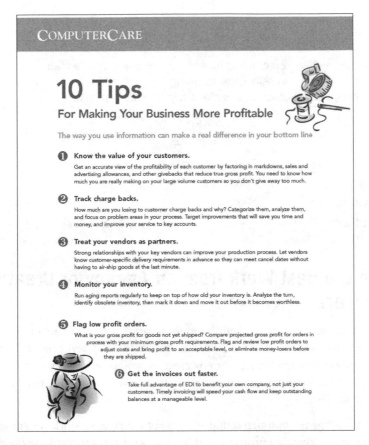

Figure 6.1 *ComputerCare sells ERP inventory management software to mid-sized apparel importers and manufacturers. These businesses are eager to improve their profitability. So, a two-page "10 tips" document on the subject is attractive to them. ComputerCare uses the document as an offer in lead-generation campaigns and as collateral material for sales calls and trade show booths.*

There is one place where information offers don't work: the executive suite. The most senior managers, the CEOs, CIOs, and CFOs (known as the "C" level) are less responsive to information offers than their underlings, who, presumably, are the ones gathering the information to make the business case for the purchase decision. What works best for the C-level, according to Cyndi Greenglass, president of Diamond Marketing Solutions in Chicago, are premiums. Not t-shirts, but gadgets and toys, such as a set of golf balls or a remote-control robot.

But the execs are the exception. The rule is still the rule. Go for the information-based offer for best results in B-to-B.

B-TO-B INFORMATION OFFER CHECKLIST

Information offers come in all kinds of sizes, shapes, and formats. To stimulate your thinking, consider the following types of information content that have been used successfully as offers to stimulate response:

Analyst report	Research report
Article reprint	Seminar or webinar
Book	"Ten Tips" brochure
Case studies	Video or CD
Newsletter	White papers
Product demo	

Getting the Best Work from an Agency or Creative Freelancers

Many lead generators buy marketing communication services from an outside agency or a freelancer, rather than employ copywriters and designers in-house. If you are working with outsiders—or any creative professionals for that matter—there are certain steps you can take to motivate their best work. In short, you want to be a great client.

In B-to-B lead-generation marketing, the goal of the creative work is to motivate a response from a qualified prospect, and then move that prospect along the sales continuum to closure. So it's imperative that you hire professionals who have experience in:

- Direct marketing communications, which are more of a science than an art.

- B-to-B direct marketing, which is somewhat different from consumer direct marketing in that it involves persuading a bunch of involved individuals who are taking action on behalf of their companies

After you have selected your agency or freelance partners, it's time for you to get your own house in order. Here are useful guidelines for how to get great work, developed by Robert Hacker, founder of the Hacker Group in Seattle:

- **Give your agency or vendor clear program direction.** Don't just copy the advertising or general campaign objectives and hand them to your lead-generation team. Campaign objectives are often much too broad—and frequently irrelevant—to the direct marketing mission. Be sure you address these vital questions: What are the specific goals and objectives for this particular program? How many inquiries, qualified leads, and sales do you expect? How do you want to trap leads and inquiries? What is the proper way to transmit the inquiries and leads into the selling system?

- **Keep the marketing mission focused.** The death knell of many programs starts with the following statement, *"As long as we're going to send them a package, why don't we..."* Every time you pile on another objective, your chance of hitting your primary objective—generating a lead, for example—falls dramatically.

- **Write cogent, well-reasoned program strategies and get them approved internally before you engage outside resources.** Get all the team input you need, and then write a campaign brief. Get the brief approved by the team before you give it to your agency or vendor. If you don't have time to write it, make your agency or vendor do it, but then get it approved internally before you start creative work. This document becomes the "touchstone" you use to bring both internal and external resources back to focus on the specific mission.

- **Manage expectations.** In a typical lead-generation program, a client might measure the initial response rate, the qualified lead rate, presentations made, and sales closed. Make sure the expected rates are communicated to all parties in advance. This avoids surprises later.

- **Understand and communicate your internal constraints and systems.** Every program should be planned around your internal and system constraints. Here are a few examples: What are your web-based marketing capabilities? What kind of systems support can you expect from IT, and what will you have to outsource? What are your inbound and outbound telemarketing capabilities? Are there volume constraints? What are your fulfillment capabilities? Think about your field-selling organization. How many leads can they handle effectively? How do they define a qualified lead? What is the proper way to deliver that lead? Make sure your agency has all the information you do.

- **Manage and control your team.** Teams are generally in place today, instead of a single program "champion," raising the question of who is running the project. Teams are fine, as long as somebody is willing to take responsibility for managing the team and take ultimate responsibility for decision making. The team leader must protect your agency or vendor from team dynamics, just as your agency or vendor must protect the client from its own internal oddities. When it comes to team input on copyediting, for example, it's much better when the team leader sorts out the good edits from the bad, and then forwards a single edited document to the agency, versus forwarding all edits to the agency for sorting out. The result is faster and much less expensive.

- **Collect all relevant data for proper response analysis.** Collect data at each conversion step—response rates, qualifying rates, field transmittal rates, and so on. If you measure every step in the selling system, you can see what works and what doesn't. Then create reports that can get everybody on the team to have the same view of how the program works. You need to counter the anecdotes with facts.

- **Simplify the approval process.** The more people in the loop, the worse program performance gets. Why? Great programs are created by a writer and designer who have unique insights into how to influence strangers at long distance. They know, for example, that changing a word or two, or making a specific emotional appeal, can double or triple response rates. The greater the number of people who review and approve program, the greater the chance that edits will take away that advantage.

- **Reduce the size of program development teams.** If you can't reduce the size of the team, change the roles and responsibilities so that not all team members get input and veto power. One person must take ultimate responsibility for program performance; the rest should support that individual with resources and information.

- **Keep detailed program performance records.** If you don't, all the money and time your company invests in lead generation will be wasted. You will be doomed to repeat the failures of the past. Share performance data with your agency or freelancers.

The direct marketing agency Rapp Collins provides guidelines for success working with sensitive creative professionals. Your agency will love working with you if you...

- Don't let your first comments be negative.

- Phrase your concerns as questions.

- Share your concerns honestly, and then let the creative team figure out how to solve them.

- Put yourself in the prospect's shoes when looking at the concept.

Your agency will *not* like working with you if...

- You change your mind between the brief and presentation.

- Take a Chinese menu approach: "Let's use the image from this concept and the copy from that concept."

- Ask your spouse or admin which concept he or she likes best.

- Set up a chaotic approval process that results in endless changes.

- Fail to support work you approved when showing it to your higher ups.

7

Response Planning and Management

A lead-generation campaign is composed of two parts: planning the campaign and managing the responses that come in as a result. Sometimes, the first part is called the front end and the second, the back end. Different companies use different terms and conventions, but to most marketers, there's no ambiguity about which part is sexier, cooler, or more fun. The front end—where creative strategies, compelling offers, eye-catching graphics, and snappy winning messages are crafted—wins hands down.

But surprise: The boring old back end is where your business future lives. The back end has so much leverage that even small improvements can have immediate, significant results on the return on investment (ROI) of lead generation.

Response management is where business begins: the business of generating an inquiry, converting it into a qualified lead, and eventually converting the prospect into a (credit) card-carrying, revenue-producing customer.

In fact, if you develop and execute a solid response management plan, it not only pulls your company ahead in the marketplace but it also makes you a hero. Make response management an essential part of your campaign by developing systems, putting people in place, and setting aside at least 10 percent of your campaign budget to pay for fulfillment and qualification. You will need more to fund lead nurturing.

Response Management Step-by-Step

Response management involves the following steps:

1. Response capture.

2. Inquiry fulfillment.

3. Inquiry qualification.

4. Hand off to sales.

5. Tracking to closure.

In this chapter, we focus on response capture and inquiry fulfillment. We discuss the remaining steps in Chapter 8, "Lead Qualification."

Six Strategies to Capture the Response Data You Need

The point of a lead-generation campaign is not to generate a mass of random, unactionable campaign responses. Of course, you want the highest number of inquiries possible, but *quality* is of the utmost importance. You need enough data to allow assessment of potential value to the company, fulfillment of the inquiry, and nurturing of the relationship until the inquiry can be converted into a real, live, paying customer.

Use these six strategies to track and capture response data:

1. **Capture the code.** All outbound communications should include a key code. This can be a "priority code" number in the letter or on the response device, a pixel buried in an email, a special extension after an 800 number, or a special URL or URL extension address. Make sure you have systems and procedures in place to capture and record the codes well in advance of the campaign drop date. Also make sure that the teams handling the responses—whether they're internal call centers or outsourced fulfillment companies—are well-informed, well-trained and

motivated to capture as many codes as possible to optimize your campaign tracking.

 Tip

Despite your best efforts, a certain amount of inbound responses will inevitably remain unconnected to an outbound campaign. You can make the connection using "data matchback," where the final buyer list is compared to the list of prospects receiving the messages.

2. **Provide more media options.** Unless you have a reason to limit the response to certain media, make every communication channel available for your prospects' responding convenience. Make it easy for them to respond by phone, Web, business reply card, fax, email, and so on. More media options mean higher response rates.

3. **Pick up the postage.** Use prepaid business reply mail for mail-in cards or envelopes. Design mail-in forms also to be faxable, and don't forget to include the fax number.

4. **Get personal.** Personalize or pre-populate your reply forms wherever possible with the prospect's name, company name, and address. This ensures accuracy, improves key code capture, and saves the prospect time in completing the form.

5. **Qualify.** Include qualification questions on response forms—where appropriate—whether printed or digital. For an example of this, see Figure 7.1. Just keep in mind that, while asking for more data can reduce the expense of outbound qualification later, it also reduces campaign response. (For more on inquiry qualification, see Chapter 8.)

6. **Schedule campaign drops.** To create a smooth inflow of responses, which reduces pressure on the response handlers and regulates the lead flow to the sales team, schedule your campaign drops carefully. Consider the likely response flow, which will be fast from digital media and slower from mail. If possible, break your campaign into batches, so the inflow of inquiries is smoother.

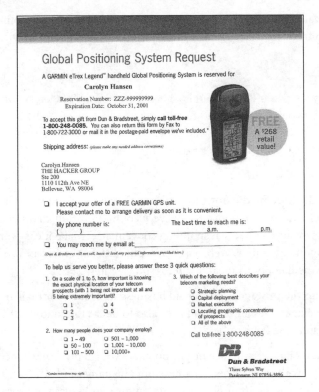

Figure 7.1   *This response form from a direct mail package does everything right. The respondent's information is pre-populated on the form, along with the key code, and the form includes multiple response media options and three important qualification questions. Used with permission of the Hacker Group.*

 Tip

> To interrogate your processes, see what they look like from a customer's viewpoint. Pretend to be an inquirer and see how you are treated. This technique is sometimes called "mystery shopping." It's also a good idea to test the processes of your competitors by responding to their campaigns, and then make sure yours are stronger in every way.

The All-Important Landing Page

To increase conversion rates in an online marketing campaign, nothing beats an effective landing page. Not to be confused with a home page, which should serve only as a starting point for visitors to search your website, a landing page is both the first stop and final destination. Once visitors are deposited there from a hot link or ad, they should never have to leave—except to move on to the sales conversion process that the landing page is designed to drive. This one page should contain everything needed to take the action you want: make a purchase, opt in to email, read content, supply information, or whatever your campaign objectives dictate.

However, not all landing pages are created equal. Some deliver, and some fall far short. How can you create the kind of knockout landing pages that produce killer conversion rates?

Features That Make for Happy Landings

The best landing pages use a clean, uncluttered design to showcase these five features:

1. **Tightly focused information.** Effective landing pages supply detailed information about *only* the specific product or service that generated enough interest to make the user want to pay a visit in the first place. They do not attempt to sell a whole catalog of products or wax eloquent about a company. Your copy should be finely crafted to give your prospect a reason to take an action or convert and address any obstacles or objections to doing so. It should also include ample keywords to improve search engine optimization. Keep it simple, with a single message and an easy-to-read design.

2. **A clear call to action.** A landing page has one purpose: to make someone do something. If it doesn't produce the desired action, it's a failure. Period. Make it easy for visitors to act by using a clearly labeled, highly visible call to action, such as a clickable button. (Research shows large red buttons work best.)

3. **A one-page display with the important elements above the fold.** According to website optimization firm Interactive Marketing Inc., using a single page can increase conversion by 55 percent. Single page or not, all main information and the call to action should be visible "above the fold," or without the need to scroll down. That's where users spend the vast majority of time. (If you need to take more space, make sure you repeat the call to action below the fold and on all subsequent pages.)

4. **An irresistible headline.** Conventional wisdom says a reader spends two seconds reading a headline. No time to spare! Keep words and phrases consistent with those used on the original link, so visitors don't waste a millisecond wondering if they've landed in the right place.

5. **Self-segmentation.** Invite landing page visitors to identify their interests around products, or their characteristics, such as whether they are a smallor medium business or a large enterprise, or what industry they work in. Then, provide a dedicated set of next steps based on this segmentation, designed to convert them in a customized path.

 Tip

To make sure visitors know they've arrived in the right spot, repeat keywords or phrases from the ad that brought them there.

One or Many Landing Pages?

If one landing page is good, many landing pages can be even better. A best practice is to create dedicated landing pages customized to the original marketing message, the target audience or the desired result: to make a purchase, to supply information, or to read or download content. In a pay-per-click (PPC) search marketing campaign (such as Google AdWords), you can create a variety of landing pages optimized to correspond with the keywords used by the searcher. PPC search "dynamic change" pages actually change based on the term that is clicked. (One recent dynamic change test done by Marketing Sherpa produced more than a 48 percent lift in conversions, plus a higher average order value per customer ordering from that page.)

WHEN GOOD HEADLINES GO BAD

A series of tests conducted by Marketing Experiments shows that the right landing page headline can increase conversion rates by 73 percent or more. The wrong headline can be disastrous. In certain cases, the difference between "right" and "wrong" can be as few as two words.

For a client selling software solutions, Marketing Experiments tested two variations of a headline:

- Say Yes when a client asks you to review FIVE MILLION separate documents.

- Say Yes when a client asks you to review FIVE MILLION separate documents. And smile.

Headline 1 produced a 0.95 percent conversion rate. Headline 2 was a complete failure, producing not a single lead.

Determine What Data Elements to Capture

There is an inverse relationship between quantity and quality in lead generation. This maxim is particularly apparent when it comes to landing page data capture decisions. Simply put, the more data fields you ask for—especially the more data fields you require with an asterisk—the lower your conversion rates and the higher the quality of the possible lead because you have more data to work with, and because the prospect has demonstrated stronger interest by having filled in more fields.

There are no simple rules to guide your data capture decisions. You need to determine the right number of data elements as well as the most important data fields that are essential to capture. You might begin considering this matter with a philosophical discussion. What is the objective of your lead-generation campaign? In most large enterprises, lead volume is not the objective. The objective is to *generate enough qualified leads so that each sales territory is optimally busy, productive, and fulfilling its quota.* Delivering too many leads can be as wasteful as delivering too few. Your goal is to find among the inquirers those whose pocketbooks are open, who have a budget, who have a business problem to solve—now—and who can influence or make a purchase decision.

It boils down to your marketing strategy. Are you looking to gather up as many contacts as possible, build your database, and market to them later? If so, keep the number of data fields to an absolute minimum. But if you are looking to gather qualified leads right off the bat, or you only want to deal with certain types of targets, and you have no interest in marketing to people outside that target, then ask for every necessary data element on the response form. Consider the example of RightNow Technologies, which offers call center technology as a service to large enterprises. For large-enterprise lead generation, RightNow is only interested in connecting with prospects at companies that are likely to need their service, such as Fortune 1000 or above. So their landing page, pictured in Figure 7.2, contains a long list of qualifying questions about company size and buying process stage, perfectly fitting their strategic marketing objectives.

To help you think this through, here are some points to consider:

- What is the purpose of the form in your marketing strategy?

- How important is quality versus quantity of campaign responses?

- What fields are necessary to making a sale?

- Is your offer substantial enough to justify the data elements being requested?

- Can you get the data elements another way, for example, in a follow-up communication?

Figure 7.2   *Used with the permission of RightNow Technologies.*

Placement Counts

It's not just what you say on your landing page, it's where you place it. According to Eyetrack III, one in a series of studies of online readers conducted by the Poynter Institute, readers fix first on the upper left area of the page. They are also immediately drawn to headlines, especially in the upper left, with larger headlines receiving more attention than smaller ones. The study also showed that underlined headlines and visual breaks such as a line or a rule tend to discourage visitors from reading beyond the break.

Tip

Each sales lead can cost hundreds or thousands of dollars to generate, but each can generate thousands or even millions of dollars in sales. You know that, but the rest of the company might not be so aware. Communicate the average value of a lead to sales reps, call centers, and all around the company. Suggest senior managers refer to leads as "valuable," and compensate your salespeople on lead follow-up rates.

Why Responses Are Often Mishandled

When a company is investing time and money in lead-generating activities, it can be frustrating to learn that inquiries sometimes go unanswered by marketers, and that leads might be ignored by the sales team. There are a number of reasons why this happens:

- Response management processes may be flawed.

- Marketers get caught up in the glamour of outbound campaigning and devote insufficient energy and resources to the "back end" of inquiry management.

- Sales people have a natural inclination to focus on current customers instead of pursuing new business.

- Sales is unable to make contact with the prospect after several attempts and then condemns the lead as poor quality.

- Prior experience with poor quality leads from marketing has left sales people uncomfortable with investing more time in new leads.

- Sales receives more leads than they can handle, so they cherry pick the ones they like and toss the rest.

There are several methods for combating this problem:

- Inspect your response capture processes. Are inquiries falling through the cracks? Are your response forms properly designed, online and offline? An excellent example of a well-designed paper-based response form used by booth workers at trade show exhibits for King Industries, a specialty chemical manufacturer, appears in Figure 7.3. King focuses on product interest as the primary qualification criterion. The form has been designed to be filled out easily, with check boxes and pre-printed answer options.

- Report regularly on conversion rates. Remember, if it's not measured, it won't be managed.

- Spot check the system. Once a month, or more often, track a sample response as it makes its way through the company to observe the process, identify any weaknesses, and make improvements. Do the same with your competitors, to find out what your customers are experiencing elsewhere.

- Involve the sales team in lead-generation planning and execution. Communicate regularly, and tailor the program to meet the sales people's requirements.

Staple Imprint or Business Card Here

Make sure you have:
Shipping Address for Samples
ie: No PO Boxes
And Phone Numbers

2002 ICE Lead Form

KING INDUSTRIES SPECIALTY CHEMICALS

GENERAL INFORMATION - Please Circle

DAY: **Wed.** **Thurs.** **Fri.**

TIME: 9-10 10-11 11-12 12-1
1-2 2-3 3-4 4-5

TAKEN BY: FAK PMB RB WJB ROB LJC
RDC CRF CHF JJF SJK SLK MAM DJM
RR RJS
Name (Reps etc.)______________________

CUSTOMER INFO: A B C

Product	Product #'s	Sample	Literature	Other
NACURE & K-CURE				
K-FLEX				
K-SPERSE				
K-KAT				
NACORR				
DISPARLON				
K-STAY				
CURENOX/SAMCURE				
NEW GEN. BROCH.				
OTHER______				

Remarks:

Figure 7.3 *Used with the permission of Bob Burk, CTSM, King Industries, Inc.*

Inquiry Fulfillment: The Beginning of a Beautiful Relationship

All right, nicely done! The campaign has dropped successfully and the inquiries are flowing in at a brisk, satisfying pace. Pat yourself on the back, and then get ready to get busy. What you do or do not do right now can either start a valuable relationship or destroy these budding connections and render your campaign investment worthless.

Because Inquiring Minds Want to Know...

If you've followed Strategy #2 from the previous section, inquiries will come in through a number of media sources. You need to be prepared with a process to capture them so they can be fulfilled, qualified, and managed properly, regardless of source.

Table 7.1 lists typical sources and tips for capturing the information according to source.

Table 7.1   Inquiry Capture by Response Medium

Response Medium	Planning Tips
Mail, including business reply mail	Even if most respondents use phone or Internet for their replies, don't eliminate the mail option from your campaign. Invariably, some prospects prefer to use the old-fashioned response method.
Phone, via an 800 number or your company office number	Scripts must be in place to capture qualifying information and source code. It is also important that the call center be open during business hours, serving all time zones where customers do business.
Fax	The fact is fax is decreasing in importance as a business communications tool. But if you offer a fax response option, set up a dedicated fax line for responses, so they don't get mingled with regular business communications.
Email	Like phone and fax, email brings with it an expectation of fast turn-around.
Web response form	When using electronic outbound media, such as email, banners, or search engine ads, the web response form is connected automatically to the message. For offline media, choose a URL that is easy to type to improve capture rates. Beware of using your own website URL alone because it won't permit tracking.
Scribbled notes from sales contacts	Salespeople might be loath to share contacts they make at events and other interactions, so regularly hounding them to submit them is a good practice.

If inbound channels are under separate management in your company, it's up to you to bring everyone together to help you design a system that works for all parties involved. Smooth coordination between the call center, the Internet team, and the mail handlers will serve your customers well and generate feelings of buy-in and team spirit.

Three Key Steps in Inquiry Handling

Regardless of inquiry source, you must take the following three actions with every campaign response:

1. **Log the inquiry into a database.** Use your dedicated lead-management database if you have one or the general marketing database. Match the

inquiry against prior sales and marketing contacts to make sure it is not a duplicate. Capture the qualification criteria from the response.

2. **Screen it.** If the qualification questions on the response form provide enough information to identify the lead as sales rep-ready, the lead should immediately move to the hand-off process. The rest of the inquiries need to flow to qualification. Noncampaign generated inquiries, such as those that come from publicity or over the transom, will have no additional information. They need to be qualified from scratch. (For more about lead qualification, see Chapter 8.)

3. **Fulfill it with the appropriate materials.** You should have prepared collateral materials specific to the campaign, but you also need to be ready with appropriate materials for noncampaign-generated inquiries. Traditionally, inquiries were fulfilled with a direct mail piece. These days, the more likely fulfillment method is an email with a link to downloadable collateral material—or a web link that pops up on the acknowledgment page after the web response form is completed.

 Tip

Learn from your market responses when it comes to fulfillment material planning. Develop your best informational materials on the products or services that receive the most inquiries. Develop an alternative generic product or company brochure as a catch-all.

Six Rules of Fullfillment

You made a promise in your campaign, and your prospect is expecting you to deliver on that promise—whether it's to send out a white paper or to follow up with a phone call. Planning carefully for fast and error-free fulfillment is essential to campaign success. Here are six principles to keep in mind:

1. **Speed is of the essence.** Now that you have someone's interest, strike while the iron is hot! Research shows that the faster fulfillment materials are received, the more likely the lead is to be qualified. The need is still fresh, and competitors are less likely to be in the way. Aim for a 24-hour turnaround on printed materials, and instantaneous response on digital materials. To help you plan, consider these points:

   - Your processes better be well-designed and working smoothly. Test them, mystery shop them, and refine them regularly.

- Fulfill with web-based collateral material where possible. This format is not only fast, but it is infinitely flexible. You can update and customize to the individual inquirer's need. Develop a library of downloadable collateral, such as white papers, case studies, research reports, and presentations, all in PDF or other easy-to-share, viral-friendly formats.

- If an inquiry rests on someone's desk "till they get to it," your system will fail. Motivate the staff to make response-handling a top priority. Track response time to inquiry fulfillment along with volume and quality of responses.

2. **Relevance rules: Don't think kitchen sink.** With the delicious prospect of fresh interest, you may be tempted to throw additional product brochures and anything else you have lying around into the fulfillment package. Resist! Your package will end up appearing disorganized and unprofessional. Remember, the purpose of the materials is to move the prospect closer to a sale, as part of what is likely to be a long series of interactions over time. You want your fulfillment materials to have as much relevance to the original inquiry as possible—even making it pick up the look and feel of the original. This provides consistency, reinforces your brand's image and increases the package's perceived relevance and value.

3. **What to do about duplicates.** Duplicate entries are common and often unintentional—respondents simply forget they've already expressed interest. So you need to de-duplicate all inquiries against your database. When you do find a duplicate, consider developing a less expensive fulfillment package to satisfy the inquiry without breaking the bank. If you are using web-based fulfillment, you can just let them download collateral to their hearts' content, but you should acknowledge to the prospect that the connection has already been made, and welcome them back. If the original inquiry has been qualified and is in the hands of a sales person, notify the rep of the fresh inquiry.

4. **Cull out the suspects.** Look for competitors, students, librarians, and other information seekers who are unlikely to be true sales prospects. Send them the same bare-bones fulfillment package as the duplicates—or ignore them altogether.

5. **Stimulate usage.** You want your fulfillment materials opened as soon as possible, so be sure to communicate that the materials are expected, to serve as a memory trigger for the recipient and create a sense of urgency. A message in the email subject line or on the outer envelope, such as "Here are the materials you requested," will do the trick.

6. **Use personalization.** You want this to be the beginning of a beautiful relationship, so give it a warm start. Personalize your response in a way that shows how valuable you consider this prospect and hints of the individualized attention he or she can expect from your company in all future dealings.

 Tip

Consider further qualifying the prospect by telephoning in advance of sending the fulfillment package. This enables you to find out more about the specific information he needs and further personalize your cover letter.

WHAT GOES INTO A FULFILLMENT PACKAGE?

Most B-to-B marketers today use digital downloads for delivering fulfillment material. But some still find that a printed and mailed package can work wonders at getting past gatekeepers and serving as ongoing reference materials of value to the prospect. If you decide to use printed materials, here's a list of important components that can make the package work as hard as it can to move your prospect along the buying process.

Printed fulfillment packages typically include the following components:

- An outer envelope announcing the arrival of the materials requested.

- A short, personalized cover letter that acknowledges the prospect's expression of interest, describes the package contents and their purpose, and tells the prospect what to do next.

- Sales materials filled with eye-catching devices such as sticky notes or hand-written margin notes. Include information on where to buy, such as a list of local dealers or contact information for the sales rep in the territory.

- An involvement device, like a survey, or a checklist of product features and benefits.

- Packaging that encourages the customer to hold on to the materials, such as a file folder.

- A response device and instructions for what to do next. This can be a business reply envelope (BRE), a business card with your contact information, or a Rolodex card—whatever allows the customer to take some action to keep in touch with you.

It's a Large Party in Response Management

Round up the input and the cooperation of the wide variety of parties who have an interest in response management in your organization. Here's a checklist of possible people to include, from lead-management expert James W. Obermayer, founder of the Sales Lead Management Association.

The departments and labor services involved in inquiry management include:

- **Agencies.** Advertising, public relations, direct marketing and online service agencies create demand through all of the traditional lead-generation tactics. They have an interest in the outcome. They also drive response into a receptacle that they control: a website landing page or telemarketing contact center.

- **Electronic inquiry nurturing service organizations** that follow predetermined pathways for sending email communications to the not-ready-for-a-sales-call inquirers. Examples include marketing automation software and an ASP provider.

- **Inbound telemarketing** (taking toll-free calls), which typically reports to sales, marketing, or both.

- **Inquiry qualification departments.** These can be inside the company or with an outside vendor. While the business rules governing the pursuit of a qualified lead varies, these people call inquirers to qualify and nurture them. In the process, they eliminate students, competitors, and other illegitimate inquiries, like prisoners

- **Outbound lead-generation department.**

- **Inside sales.**

- **Marketing.**

- **Marketing communications.**

- **Sales operations.**

- **Field (sales) marketing managers**, especially those who have developed some frustration with marketing departments that do not generate enough demand.

- **Sales channel management.**

- **Demand management department**, which may report to sales or marketing. This is also known as the inquiry management department.

- **Data entry**, which can be in sales or marketing.

- **Warehousing for collateral**, which includes picking and packing literature packages (includes a letter, literature, technical data sheets, business
  reply device, dealer locations, and so on) and mailing the package.

- **Printing vendor.** In addition to printing collateral, printers might warehouse and ship your literature individually or in bulk quantities to
  resellers.

- **Direct mail houses** that might warehouse and ship your literature to
  inquirers or in bulk to resellers.

- **IT services. Internal** for software hosting, report generation, program-
  ming for sales force automation, and contact management.

- **IT services. External**, including ASP software/services provider, sales
  force automation software, contact management, and CRM.

- **Outsourced inbound and outbound telemarketing facilities.**

- **Outsourced bulk literature distribution facilities** within your own
  company. Literature distribution is often a corporate department servic-
  ing the needs of many far-flung business units.

- **Inquiry management vendors.** Includes advertising agencies that do
  this work, telemarketing firms, printers, fulfillment vendors, and direct
  mail vendors that do it part-time.

- **International offices** that might have to mimic the domestic operations for all of the previous.

8

Lead Qualification

To borrow a page from Law and Order, when it comes to business-to-business (B-to-B) lead generation, marketing and sales have separate, yet equally important roles to play. Marketing provides qualified leads to sales, and then sales works the leads until they convert to revenue or are declared otherwise resolved. This division of labor increases sales force productivity by ensuring they're not wasting time with unqualified leads or prospects who are never going to buy.

However, the system works only if marketing thinks quality, not quantity, in generating leads. You do not want to send every possible lead over to sales. The objective is to generate enough qualified leads so that each sales territory is optimally busy, productive, and fulfilling its quota. Separate the wheat from the chaff: Eliminate the inquirers who are merely browsing or doing research. Your sales people want prospects who have money in their budgets, a business problem to solve now, and the influence or authority to make a purchase decision.

Setting Qualification Criteria: Can't Beat BANT

How do you determine qualification criteria? Your best resource is in-house, perhaps right down the hall: It's your sales force. After all, they are the ones who will be handling each lead and taking it to closure. Your salespeople know better than anyone the nature of the sales process and what kind of buying characteristics are most likely to be workable for them. Follow their lead on leads!

As a general rule, many B-to-B qualification strategies are based on criteria involving one or all of the following four categories, often collectively shortened to BANT:

- **Budget.** Is the purchase budgeted, and what amount of money is available? You will want to set up categories or ranges for easier scoring. Some sellers request information about the prospect company's credit history.

- **Authority.** Does the respondent have the internal authority to make the purchase decision? If not, try to capture information about additional relevant contacts.

- **Need.** How important is the product or solution to the company, and how deep is their pain? This criterion might be difficult to ask directly, but it can be approached indirectly with questions such as: "What is the problem to be solved?" "What alternative solutions are you considering?" "What product do you currently use?" "How many do you need?"

- **Time frame.** When will the customer be able to buy? Depending on industry and sales cycle length, this can be broken into days, months, or even years. Also be sure to ask whether the customer would like to talk to a salesperson.

In addition to BANT, you may have other criteria based on your targeted company and industry. Some common ones are:

- **Potential sales volume.** How many departments in your target companies might use this product? How much of or how often might they need the product?

- **Predisposition to buy from you.** Are they past customers? Are they similar to your current customers? Would they recommend you to their colleagues?

- **Account characteristics.** What is the target company size, both in terms of revenue and number of employees? Is this a parent company or part of a larger organization? If part of a larger organization, where is the buying decision made?

Ultimately, the criteria you use need to serve your particular business. You may find that the standard criteria that work for many companies might not represent your best choice. So think strategically about your customer's buying process, and get creative with your possible criteria options.

Here's an example. King Industries, a specialty chemicals manufacturer, knows that a sale is not going to happen unless the prospect requests a sample of the product so their lab technicians can experiment with it, to be sure the chemical works in the process at hand. So King's number one qualifier is "Requested a sample." A "yes" answer to that question automatically elevates the inquiry to qualified, and the lead is handed off to sales.

What to Ask and When to Ask It

The best way to develop qualification questions is to set the criteria in concert with your sales team. Sit down with a couple of sales managers or a few top sales reps. Don't take everything they say as gospel—or they'll insist that you deliver only leads that are going to close tomorrow. Spend some time with a sales manager or a few senior experienced sales reps, and ask them to describe their ideal prospect. You might ask them for five critically important, must-have characteristics to qualify and pursue a prospect. Select from the picture they paint the categories that will be the most productive—and those where you can realistically gather the information—and then determine the range of answers that fit their needs.

Here's how such a conversation might go with a sales force charged with selling enterprise-wide licensing deals for a file-sharing software-as-a-service. You say, "Describe your ideal prospect." They say, "We want to find a strategic, visionary person, who wants to have an impact on the business and understands that enterprise software is moving to the cloud." How can you convert this description to a reasonable set of qualifying questions? Based on what you have so far, not easily. You need to back up and probe further. So you might ask questions like:

- How big an enterprise are you looking for? How many employees? What kind of revenue levels?

- What industries are you targeting? Have you gotten traction in particular industries?

- What titles are these visionary people likely to have?

You know it's difficult to assess the prospect's vision or aptitude for innovation with a standard question. So in this case, it is likely more productive to ask questions about the current environment. For example, a yes/no question about whether the target company is using cloud-based software anywhere in the corporation might be a reasonable proxy for the degree of new-technology adoption and, in fact, a strong indicator that another cloud-based application might find a home there. The final list of qualification questions might be around company size, industry and current cloud computing usage.

Some other tips for success with qualification questions:

- Ask your qualification questions on your response forms, whether they are paper-based, by voice, or electronic. Asking questions at the point of inquiry collection will most likely reduce campaign response rates, but you can make it up in increased qualification rates, which saves money in the long run by reducing outbound qualification effort.

- Ask prospects all the questions the sales team needs to do its job. If you don't ask, your conversion rates will fall dramatically.

- Ask for the order. Include a hard option such as "Have a sales specialist contact me" as a check-off box on every form. You might even go further by asking what the best time would be for the rep to make contact.

- Set criteria that are used consistently across campaigns. Instead of developing original criteria for every campaign, try to gain agreement on a few—3 or 4—basic questions that apply across your product lines. These might be created around BANT criteria, or target company characteristics such as employee size, industry, and geography. If you can pull this off, you can analyze results over time and across campaign variables such as list, offer, and creative. This strategy also reduces confusion and extra work during campaign planning.

Adding the qualification questions to your response form reduces response, but saves much time and expense by side-stepping outbound qualification messaging. See Figure 8.1 for an example of a response vehicle in the form of a survey, courtesy of the Hacker Group, which includes more than 10 questions intended to qualify prospects. Using a survey can be an effective method when you need to capture answers to a relatively long batch of qualification questions.

Need for Speed: Moving Qualified Leads into the Pipeline

In the recent past, the phone was the best medium for lead qualification, but now email has taken the "lead" as the preferred communications channel. Sometimes, as when the prospect has provided no other contact information, direct mail is the best choice for outbound qualification communications.

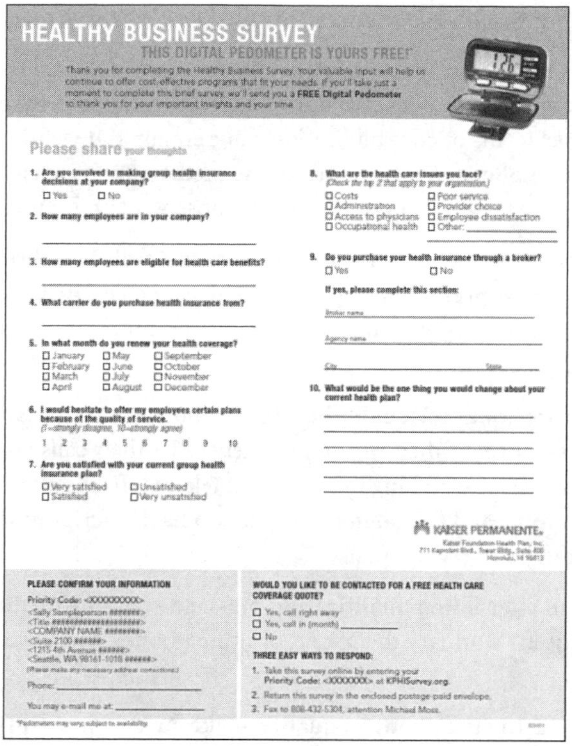

HEALTHY BUSINESS SURVEY

THIS DIGITAL PEDOMETER IS YOURS FREE!*

Thank you for completing the Healthy Business Survey. Your valuable input will help us continue to offer cost-effective programs that fit your needs. If you'll take just a moment to complete this brief survey, we'll send you a **FREE Digital Pedometer** to thank you for your important insights and your time.

Please share your thoughts

1. Are you involved in making group health insurance decisions at your company?
   ☐ Yes ☐ No
2. How many employees are in your company?
3. How many employees are eligible for health care benefits?
4. What carrier do you purchase health insurance from?
5. In what month do you renew your health coverage?
   ☐ January ☐ February ☐ March ☐ April ☐ May ☐ June ☐ July ☐ August ☐ September ☐ October ☐ November ☐ December
6. I would hesitate to offer my employees certain plans because of the quality of service.
   (1=strongly disagree, 10=strongly agree)
   1 2 3 4 5 6 7 8 9 10
7. Are you satisfied with your current group health insurance plan?
   ☐ Very satisfied ☐ Satisfied ☐ Unsatisfied ☐ Very unsatisfied
8. What are the health care issues you face?
   (Check the top 2 that apply to your organization.)
   ☐ Costs ☐ Administration ☐ Access to physicians ☐ Occupational health ☐ Poor service ☐ Provider choice ☐ Employee dissatisfaction ☐ Other: _____
9. Do you purchase your health insurance through a broker?
   ☐ Yes ☐ No
   If yes, please complete this section:
   Broker name
   Agency name
   City State
10. What would be the one thing you would change about your current health plan?

KAISER PERMANENTE.

PLEASE CONFIRM YOUR INFORMATION

Priority Code: <XXXXXXXXX>
<Sally Sampleperson #######>
<Title ####################>
<COMPANY NAME ########>
<Suite 2100 ######>
<1215 4th Avenue ######>
<Seattle, WA 98161-1018 ######>

Phone: _____

You may e-mail me at: _____

WOULD YOU LIKE TO BE CONTACTED FOR A FREE HEALTH CARE COVERAGE QUOTE?

☐ Yes, call right away
☐ Yes, call in (month) _____
☐ No

THREE EASY WAYS TO RESPOND:

1. Take this survey online by entering your Priority Code: <XXXXXXX> at KPHISurvey.org.
2. Return this survey in the enclosed postage-paid envelope.
3. Fax to 808-432-5304, attention Michael Moss.

Source: The Hacker Group

Figure 8.1 *Response vehicle in survey format.*

After inquiries are fulfilled, there's no time to dilly-dally. The processes for moving qualified leads into the pipeline need to be designed for speed and efficient handling. Some companies have the luxury of using full-time, dedicated staff. Others use employees who have other duties too. Still, others outsource the function completely. In any case, the staff needs to be motivated and compensated to encourage 100% handling of inquiries within a short, pre-determined time frame. It is crucial to fund the process appropriately to support the expected inquiry flow.

Which Leads Need Qualification?

You need to qualify:

- Inquiries that provide no information other than contact name and address.
- Inquiries where the qualification questions were filled out incompletely. (This can happen as much as 40% of the time.)

As you plan your qualification process, here are 12 key points to guide you:

1. **Email is today's preferred qualification medium.** Design your outbound qualification emails to link to a web-based qualification form. Like other forms of communication, your emails and web-based forms should also offer several other response media options, including email, but also phone, fax, and postal mail for those who prefer them.

2. **Wherever possible, direct your inquiries to a web-based response form for their preliminary qualification, especially in a high-volume environment.** Self-reporting on the web saves money for you and time for your prospect.

3. **Be realistic about telequalifying.** Today's business people are rarely at their desks. Even if they are, they're likely to let their calls go to voice mail as a way of screening them. Expect telequalification to require between three and five attempts. Be sure to have a script ready if the phone call goes to voice mail.

4. **Set up an alternating qualification message series by medium.** If email doesn't work, try the phone, or if the phone doesn't work, try email.

5. **If you're using the phone to qualify, make sure your script is more about prospects and their needs and less about your company and your products.**

6. **Set your maximum number of touches first, and base them on a reasonable number of contacts.** For instance, if the prospect is unreachable after five phone calls and five emails, call it quits.

7. **If you cannot reach a prospect, put the name back in the marketing database for re-promotion and flag the record accordingly.** If the prospect shows interest again, and you still cannot contact him or her, then it's probably unwise to invest any more time or money in pursuit.

8. **Have a Plan B.** You might find that an inquirer who simply requests company information is not ready to even be put into a qualification stream. Design a series of interim contacts that moves this kind of inquiry along toward the point where a qualification contact makes sense.

9. **Adjust the process to the customer's situation.** You can't force customers to be ready, but you can—and must—be there when they become ready.

10. **Manage inquiries on a first-in-first-out basis, so that no lead gets cold while waiting to go to sales.**

11. **Make sure your qualifiers concentrate on qualifying.** This might seem obvious, but qualifiers, especially on the phone, can sometimes slip across the line into selling. Their only job—a hugely important one—is to qualify.

12. **Customize your outbound channel to the incoming medium.** Respondents by email, web, and fax expect faster service than postal-mail users.

THREE SECRETS FOR LEAD-QUALIFICATION SUCCESS

Applying these rules to your lead-qualification program can vastly improve its effectiveness:

1. You *must* develop qualification criteria in concert with your sales team. Ask them, "What are the characteristics of an ideal lead? How would you describe someone who is ready to buy?"

2. Keep your criteria limited. Less is more. Don't ask anything for curiosity's sake.

3. Make the form easy to complete. Use ranges and check boxes.

Lead-Ranking Strategies

Obviously, all leads are not created equal. Some are going to convert to good business much more quickly than others, which means they warrant more, and more urgent attention and action. To separate leads into appropriate "buckets," most companies develop some sort of system for lead ranking or sorting, often called lead scoring.

Lead scoring systems vary widely. Some companies classify leads as "hot," "warm," or "future" leads. Some call them "hard" or "soft" leads. However you organize your system, you *should* have a system. The criteria must be set up in consultation with the sales team, and no unqualified leads should ever be passed to sales.

Easy as A, B, C, and Possibly D

There are many ways leads can be sorted, ranked, and scored. Select the system that best suits your sales team and your industry. Remember to get input from the sales team about its preferences.

One of the most common scoring strategies is a simple alphabetical ranking. Here's how this kind of system can work:

- An "A" prospect is ready to see a sales rep. Either the prospect said so (as in, "Have a sales specialist call me"), or the predefined qualification criteria for a sales call have been met.

- A "B" prospect is imminently ready to buy but still needs nurturing. This kind of prospect is close enough to a purchase that sales, not marketing, should make the contact—perhaps a telephone call to establish the relationship.

- A "C" prospect still needs nurturing, and in this case it should be done by marketing.

- A "D" inquiry is not worth nurturing. You might decide whether to put it into the marketing database for ongoing communications or toss it.

Weight and See: Lead Scoring

Beyond lead sorting, lead scoring is method of ranking leads that assigns a numerical score to each multiple-choice answer in the qualification questions, and then pushes the lead through to the appropriate next step based on the score. This approach provides great flexibility because the weightings can be changed by campaign, by product, or even by the current level of pressure to deliver fast revenues.

Table 8.1 shows an example of how a lead scoring scheme might be designed.

In this example, let's say the sales team requests that any lead with a score of 15 or more be sent to them immediately. So they would receive a lead representing an inquirer with an approved budget (5 points) of $80,000 (3 points) who is planning to buy this quarter (5 points) and who is the end user of the solution (2 points), and thus likely to be a strong influence on the purchase decision. The sales team would also receive a lead representing an inquiry from a purchasing agent (1 point) who has an urgent need (5 points) and wants to see a sales person (10 points), but does not yet have a budget approved. For this industry and this product line, the sales team has deemed these are leads they want to work on right away. Note: In this example, assume that a purchasing agent is simply an administrative function or someone who types up purchase orders but has no decision-making authority.

Table 8.1 Sample Lead-Scoring Scheme

Criterion		Score		Score		Score		Score		Score
Budget	$0–50k	2	$50–100k	3	$100–250k	4	$250k+	5		
Authority	Recommend	4	Specify	3	Use	2	Approve	5	Purchase	1
Time frame	1–3 months	5	3–6 months	3	6–12 months	1				
Have sales rep call	Yes	10	No	0						
Budgeted	Yes	5	No	0						

Scoring Based on Website Behavior

Because so much early interaction between vendor and prospect is online, a new style of lead scoring is beginning to emerge based on the actions the prospect takes during the pre-sales research, education, and relationship building stages. This strategy reflects the fact that the prospect is digging around your site, demonstrating interest, and may be ready to interact personally with a sales person.

Ardath Albee, author of *eMarketing Strategies for the Complex Sale*, recommends useful approaches in her white paper, "The Essential Marketing Automation Handbook," published by Genius.com. First, you analyze the value of each page on your website, based on customer interest as it relates to potential purchase intent. See Table 8.2 for a hypothetical grid assigning value codes to each page.

Table 8.2   Assigning Prospecting Value to Website Pages

Website Page	Point Value
Home page	1
Download content page	10
Demo page	10
Product pages	5
Customer testimonials	10
Company pages	5
News	5
Job openings	−5
All other pages	1

Source: Adapted from *The Essential Marketing Automation Handbook* by Ardath Albee.

The next step is to assign scores to the online interactions a prospect can have with you. A website designed for lead generation has multiple ways to encourage interaction, from downloads, to attending webinars, to making blog comments, to leaving behind contact information. Assess the relative value of each, broken down by its interim interactions. In Table 8.3, see an example of how a webinar attendance might be assigned weights.

Then, assign scores to web-based interactions. An example appears in Table 8.4. After these weightings are determined, do your best to track each visitor's actions and assign a cumulative score. You might not be able to capture every data point. If the visitor has not registered, the inquiry might not be actionable as a lead. But, with experimentation and refinement, this process should allow you to develop qualified leads from early website interactions for hand off to a salesperson who can take the relationship to the next level.

Table 8.3   Scoring Webinar Interactions

Webinar Interaction	Score
Registration	5
Attendance	10
Polling participation	5
Q&A participation	10
Archive views	7

Source: Adapted from *The Essential Marketing Automation Handbook* by Ardath Albee.

Table 8.4   Scoring Inquiries

Inquiry Interactions	Score
Fill in registration form	15
Opt in to receive email	10
Download content	5
Reply to emails	5
Participate in live chat	5

Source: Adapted from *The Essential Marketing Automation Handbook* by Ardath Albee.

KNOWING THE SCORE PAYS OFF

However you organize your lead scoring system, it's likely to have an impressive payoff. Recently, the marketing automation firm Eloqua studied the results of ten B-to-B companies that introduced lead scoring into their processes and came up with the findings shown in Table 8.5. These companies improved their results by 17% to 30% simply for having improved their process—without additional campaign expense involved.

Table 8.5   Improvement in Campaign Results Due to Lead Scoring

Metrics	Before Lead Scoring	After Lead Scoring	Percentage Change
Lead close rate	31%	40%	30%
Company sales	$16.8 million	$19.8 million	18%
Revenue per deal	$39,149	$45,863	17%

Qualifying Leads at a Trade Show or Event

A trade show can be an important source of business, but it takes time and attention to do it right, due to the special nature of the face-to-face interaction an event affords. An inquiry generated at a show can be a good starting point, an excellent place to begin a relationship with a prospect who might become a buyer, influencer, or specifier, or a prospect who might be a good source of referrals. It's a rich environment for initiating sales conversations, but it's rare that a visitor turns up immediately qualified to turn over to sales. Adjust your expectations and modify both your strategy and your qualification process to suit the occasion.

Because visitors won't have the time to fill out a lengthy detailed survey, concentrate on capturing the basics:

- Contact information (name, title, company, address, email, and phone number).

- Preferred method of contact.

- Agreed-upon next steps (send product information, have a sales person call, and so on).

That being said, booth staff should be encouraged to record as much information about the prospect as possible, such as a detailed account of the conversation and any insights the staffer can take away. This information becomes part of the qualification criteria and makes the next stage in the relationship easier to achieve. A variety of software solutions are available to allow you to capture the results of your qualification discussion on a computer for easy access, storage, and transfer. The data can be entered by booth staff or by booth visitors themselves. Offering touch screens, color PDAs, or attractive kiosks for data entry can improve the likelihood that attendees will complete the process.

You can develop a new set of qualification criteria for each business event or standardize your criteria across your event marketing program. Customized qualification criteria provide more relevance, especially at business events focused on specific customer segments or product categories. However, standard qualification criteria allow consistency across marketing vehicles, making data capture easier and reducing confusion and error. So there are pros and cons to either approach, but no matter which you choose, make sure that your database is set up to capture the criteria. Consider listing the questions in the order they will be slotted into the database for ease of data transfer when you get back to the office.

Marketing Checkup for Telephone-Based Lead Generation and Qualification

The phone being one of the most useful tools in B-to-B marketing, this nifty 10-point quiz was developed by Michael A. Brown, a leading expert on telephone marketing for B-to-B. Michael instructs you to rate what you do and how you do it, and then add up the points to get your score.

1. The calling lists we rent or buy are based on:

    - Demographics, such as SIC code and number of employees. 0 points.

    - Business actions, such as moves, mergers, and new processes. 1 point.

    - Affinities, such as related purchases and memberships. 1 point.

2. We get our reps ready to call and then improve their skills by:

    - Training and practice. 1 point.

    - Teaming with another rep. 0 points.

    - Throwing them on the phone. Subtract 1 point.

    - I don't know. Subtract 1 point.

3. When on the phone, our callers follow:

    - Scripts. 0 points.

    - Call/question guides. 1 point.

    - The data fields on their computer screen. Subtract 1 point.

    - Their instincts. Subtract 1 point.

4. Our supervisors and managers monitor calls and coach our reps:

    - Every day. 1 point.

    - When they can. 0 points.

    - Seldom. 0 points.

    - Never. Subtract 1 point.

    - I don't know. 0 points.

5. In how many seconds can your callers describe what your company does?

   - 5–10. 1 point.

   - 10–15. 0 points.

   - 15 and up. Subtract 1 point.

   - We're so well known, they don't have to. 1 point.

6. What portion of lead-generation calls results in substantive conversations?

   - Less than 5%. Subtract 2 points.

   - 5%–15%. Subtract 1 point.

   - 15%–25%. 0 points.

   - 25%–50%. 1 point.

   - 50% and up. 2 points.

   - I don't know. 0 points.

7. What portion of lead-generation and qualification conversations results in the prospect taking the next step in your marketing or sales process?

   - Less than 5%. Subtract 2 points.

   - 5%–15%. Subtract 1 point.

   - 15%–25%. 0 points.

   - 25%–50%. 1 point.

   - 50% and up. 2 points.

   - I don't know. 0 points.

8. After the calls, we classify our leads as:

   - Qualified or not qualified. 0 points.

   - Hot, medium, cool or A, B, and C. 0 points.

   - Rated on a point-scale according to agreed criteria. 2 points.

   - Whatever our gut and experience say. Subtract 1 point.

   - We don't classify, we just send them along. Subtract 2 points.

9. Your level of confidence that your own CEO would accept the kind of calls your reps are making:

- Slim to none. Subtract 2 points.

- Quite low. Subtract 1 point.

- So-so. 0 points.

- Pretty high. 1 point.

- Certain. 2 points.

- I don't know. Subtract 1 point.

10. Your level of confidence that your sales channel(s) will act on the leads you produce:

- Slim to none. Subtract 2 points.

- Quite low. Subtract 1 point.

- So-so. 0 points.

- Pretty high. 1 point.

- Certain. 2 points.

- I don't know. Subtract 1 point.

How to assess your score: 10 points or higher? You're looking good. Congratulations!

9 or 8? Make the tactical adjustments before your competitors force the issue for you.

7 or 6? Your lead efforts probably are mismatched to your sales requirements and almost certainly under-performing as well. Better make some big improvements.

Under 6? Stop reading this and get professional guidance right now.

The Whos and Hows of the Handoff

At the end of your qualification process, if all goes well, you will have produced a nice shiny stack of leads, gleaming like the gold they represent to your company. Now who do you give them to? And how? And how do you make sure they're followed up?

Companies typically use criteria like these to determine which sales rep gets a lead:

- **By territory.** If the lead is in a rep's territory, the decision is easy. Problems arise, however, when an internal resource (a field sales person or an inside sales rep) and a third-party resource (a distributor or business partner) are covering the same territory. Create a decision rule based on relevant criteria such as size or complexity of the opportunity for these occasions.

- **By skill or qualification.** Sales people might have specialties, such as product or industry. In this case, again, the determination must be made by decision rule.

- **By rotation.** Hand over the leads one at a time, in rotation, when reps are equally qualified and territory is not a factor.

There are a number of transfer options available:

- **Phone in the hot stuff.** If the lead is qualified over the phone, the call center can transfer the prospect to the right sales person on the spot.

- **Email.** Sending information about a lead to the sales force via email is the recommended method today. It's inexpensive, ubiquitous, and immediate.

- **Web-based systems.** Your company's intranet or CRM system can deliver leads in as timely a fashion as email.

- **Lead-management software.** Also usually web-based, the new tools for lead tracking and management allow quick sorting, transfer, and follow-up tracking.

How will you know the leads worked? Good question and a bit tough to answer. Lead follow-up is often a source of friction between sales and marketing. Sales people grumble that marketing never sends them any good leads—which unfortunately can be true, if marketers have confused quantity with quality and delivered unqualified leads. Marketing people grouse that sales wants to claim credit for *every* piece of their business, unwilling to admit that marketing actually gave them any help. ("I was already working that account," they'll say.) But sales and marketing *can* work together on this. Here are some tips for increasing the likelihood that your leads will be well received and eagerly worked by the sales team:

- **Disburse the leads immediately.** When they're hot, they're hot, but they will cool down fast if you don't act. The customer wants an answer—from you or the competition. Use electronic channels where possible.

- **Communicate, starting early.** Give salespeople copies of campaign materials, plus detailed plans about expected lead flow, by territory. If the reps are brought in early, they will expect the leads and be prepared for their arrival. Perhaps more importantly, they will be more committed psychologically to the upcoming leads.

- **Give ALL the details.** Include full qualification information with each lead: name, address, company name, telephone number, email address (if possible), and include a complete set of answers to the qualification questions. Sales reps will not likely take the trouble to ferret out a missing phone number. (Would you?)

- **Double the communication.** Send a message to the prospect at the same time you hand the lead to sales. Tell the prospect the name, title, and contact information of the rep who is on his account. Copy the rep and maybe his boss on the message.

- **Show them the money.** Insist that lead followup be clearly provided for in sales compensation plans. The goal of sales and sales management must be 100% followup of qualified leads received, within 24 to 48 hours of receipt. Sales people need to be rewarded for following this practice, and they need to be penalized when they don't.

- **Institute mutually acceptable terms and time limits.** For instance, specify that if sales does not work a lead in 24 hours, it can be withdrawn and assigned to another sales resource. Similarly, agree that if they work a lead for one week without success, they can return the lead to marketing for further nurturing.

- **Analyze the losers.** Which inquiries qualified but did not result in business? Consider their source, and use the experience as a screener for prospect selection in campaign planning. An analysis can also help point the way towards needed changes in product or pricing and serve as a starting point for an advanced training program.

- **Treat leads like gold.** Encourage the development of a culture that thinks of a qualified lead as a valuable asset—for sales, marketing, and the whole company.

Automated Lead Distribution

One of the most aggravating elements of lead-generation programs is the difficulty of determining which sales person should get which lead. Smart companies today are setting up rules-based automated lead distribution programs that enhance the work of their SFA (sales force automation) or CRM systems.

The hard part, of course, is setting up the rules in the first place. This requires a lot of what-if planning among sales people and marketers to identify the key variables and criteria for decision-making. But once that's done, then the leads flow smoothly and—most importantly—quickly, to the right sales resource.

An example comes from Linda Tenenbaum, account executive at IMI, a database marketing firm in San Jose. One IMI client, a telecommunications equipment manufacturer, created lead-distribution decision rules based on three cascading criteria:

- **Government.** Based on certain key words or government domain names, if the lead is identified as being from a federal or state government entity, it is sent directly to one of two dedicated reps who cover government accounts.

- **Key accounts.** Based on a reference table, if the lead comes from a list of key accounts, it goes directly to the call center for follow up. After the call center personnel have further qualified the lead, it goes to the rep dedicated to the account.

- **Comments.** Based on particular interest topics in the text, the lead will be handled by customer service. For example, if key words appear for products that are no longer supported by the company, an email is generated with information about where to go to find out more about that product.

Benchmarketing Lead-Management Processes

Lead qualification is a critically important element of a successful lead-generation and management program, but it takes time and effort to plan, organize and execute. If you are wondering where you stand against other B-to-B marketers, look at the results of Marketing Sherpa's 2009 benchmarking study, displayed in Table 8.6.

Table 8.6   How B-to-B Marketers Implement Best Practices

Practice	Yes, Doing Now	No, But Priority	Not Planned
Use CRM systems to manage lead process.	51%	13%	36%
Collaborate with sales to define lead qualification criteria.	45%	20%	35%
Measure lead generation contribution to revenue.	44%	25%	31%
Have system for ranking leads.	44%	18%	38%
Have lead-nurturing process.	39%	23%	38%
Have closed-loop tracking from source to close.	30%	27%	443%
Have process for retuning unclosed leads to marketing.	28%	19%	53%

Source: Marketing Sherpa B2B Marketing Benchmark Survey, 2009.

9

Lead Nurturing

In B-to-B marketing, the so-called Rule of 45 dictates that almost half of all business inquiries—45 percent—eventually result in a sale. That should spread a smile across a marketer's face, but the kicker is that in B-to-B, "eventually" can mean many months, or even as long as several years. Savvy marketers know that if they neglect prospective customers during this long buying cycle, competitors can and will swoop in and woo them away. From the earliest point in the cycle, smart marketers move the relationship forward, building trust and awareness with a series of synchronized communications known as lead nurturing.

Lead nurturing is also sometimes called lead cultivation, lead development, or lead incubation. It's about continuing the conversation that began with the initial lead generation outreach. Like a conversation, it can go in a variety of directions. It needs to be flexible and responsive to the evolving needs and interests of the prospect.

A Marketing Function with a Big Sales Benefit

Can a program that ties up staff and money for years really be worth it? You bet! A well-run lead-nurturing program has the potential to increase campaign results dramatically. Nurturing can pay off in higher revenues and larger order sizes, as shown in a recent study from Aberdeen Group. In this study, the following resulted for the best-in-class companies, defined as the top 20 percent in revenue and lead production:

- They were twice as likely to have a nurturing program in place, compared to "average" companies (the middle 50 percent of companies).

- They were 4.6 times more likely to be involved in nurturing, compared to "laggard" companies (the bottom 30 percent of companies).

- They experienced nurtured leads resulting in 47 percent larger average order sizes than non-nurtured leads.

- They achieved higher revenues, better campaign response rates, lead qualification rates, and average order sizes.

How Nurturing Pays Off in Campaign Productivity

Consider the hypothetical example in Table 9.1. In this example, an end-to-end lead management program improved campaign results four-fold. Notice how few responses (5) arrived qualified. Over twice that amount (11) were converted to qualified leads through outbound qualification, raising campaign results +300 percent. The balance was put into a nurturing process, which generated another 25 qualified leads over time for another +200 percent. Although these numbers are hypothetical, they are completely reasonable.

Table 9.1   Qualified Leads Increase with Qualification and Nurturing

Inquiry Generation	Responses	Qualified Leads
Responses generated	100	
Immediately qualified	5	5
Unqualified balance	95	
Lead management		
Lead pool	95	
Contacts reached (60%)	57	
Qualified via outbound communication (20%)	11	11
Nurturing pool	84	
Qualified via nurturing (30%)	25	25

If It's So Great, Why Don't More Companies Do It?

Given this enormous opportunity for improving campaign productivity, it's hard to understand why some companies ignore lead nurturing or don't take advantage of its power. There are several possible reasons contributing to this situation:

- Marketers caught up in the excitement of the initial lead-generation campaign might find the concept of nurturing too tedious to focus on.

- It's easy to develop the first and second nurture contacts, but it becomes increasingly difficult to develop a 6-to-9 month multicontact communication plan that takes into consideration the combinations of responders and nonresponders within a nurture program.

- There might be unresolved conflict about where nurturing fits into the sales and marketing process, who should manage it, and how it should be funded.

Who's the Boss?

Lead nurturing is so important that it should be managed as a separate function. In my opinion, this function should be controlled by marketing, not sales, although who's in charge can be a matter of considerable internal controversy. Some companies split the difference, creating specialized nurturing teams that are a lower-cost resource but still report into sales. The main objective is to avoid asking the high-priced, time-constrained sales force to conduct the heavy lifting of lead nurturing themselves—their time is better applied to selling to qualified prospects.

The Lead-Nurturing Process, Step by Step

Lead nurturing is best viewed as a process, broken down into steps, so each element can be efficiently planned and effectively executed. Typical steps include:

1. Qualify sales inquiries via outbound contact, usually email or phone, to separate the qualified leads from the nonqualified prospects. Sources of leads requiring nurturing include:

    a. Partially qualified inquiries. They are not ready to deliver to sales, according to pre-defined qualification criteria.

    b. Leads returned by the sales team. Frequently, a presumably qualified lead turns out to require further nurturing. The contact might change jobs, or the business need might change. So, sales returns the lead to marketing for further followup.

2. Sort the remaining nonqualified prospect into buckets, based on quali-
    fication criteria, such as:

    a. Time frame to purchase

    b. Size of opportunity

    c. Whether the purchase is budgeted

    d. Job title or buying role

    e. Whether the respondent would like to see a sales rep

3. Profile the responders to gain insight into their needs and the business
    issues that are most relevant to them. As the nurturing process gathers
    new information about the inquirer, those data points must be entered
    into the database.

4. Set up a decision-tree process for communicating with the prospects by
    segment. According to Marketo, the marketing automation firm, the
    ideal segmentation for nurturing begins with industry, then company
    size, and finally buying role. The series of communications can vary
    widely, using all communications media and all kinds of sequencing
    and timing strategies.

5. When a prospect is ready to see a sales person, hand the qualified lead
    off to sales.

Mix Up the Communications Media

Nurturing can be done with all kinds of messages via all kinds of media. Consider
some of the following tactics:

- Email newsletter
- Outbound telephone call
- Event invitation (seminar, trade show, webinar)
- New product announcement
- Press release
- Online video
- Tweets
- Blogging
- Online community forum
- Catalog mailing
- Survey or market research questionnaire
- Podcast

- White paper
- Case study
- Reprint
- eBook
- Personal communication (holiday or birthday card)
- Letter from the CFO or other senior executives or from various departments (customer service or relevant area, such as IT or engineering)

As you can see in Table 9.2, the hands-down winner for nurturing media is email, followed by direct mail and telephone, according to a study by the Aberdeen Group. (Note that this is in sharp contrast to email's poor performance with cold prospects.)

Table 9.2   Top Three Media Channels for Nurturing Programs

Medium	Number of Respondents Using
Email	65%
Direct mail	44%
Telephone	26%

Source: Aberdeen Group

The Acknowledgment Page as an Early Nurturing Touch

Using web-based response forms provides a welcome opportunity to continue the interaction with carefully selected messaging on the acknowledgment page that pops up after the response form is submitted. According to Howard J. Sewell of Spear Marketing Group, you can use the acknowledgment page in a variety of ways:

- Make an offer of additional content related to the one that drove the response in the first place.
- Recruit blog subscriptions, Twitter followers, or Facebook fans.
- Encourage pass-along to colleagues.

Nurturing Best Practices

Lead nurturing can provide significant leverage to lead-generation campaigns, tripling or quadrupling campaign productivity, getting you more new customers, market share, and revenue. But in order to maximize your nurturing effort, take advantage of the best practices in nurturing today, namely, a thoughtful communications strategy, robust content development, a tracking and measurement process, and triggered communications.

Communications Strategy

Nurturing may be a prolonged effort, but it is emphatically *not* a prolonged sales pitch. Successful nurturing means keeping your company's name, expertise, products, and services "front and center" with your leads without being annoying or intrusive. Nurturing is not selling; it's relationship building.

Use these three strategies to keep your communications on the right track:

- Ensure that your communications are useful, relevant, and unique. For example, when nurturing a relationship with a technical buyer, your communications should provide details about product functionality and performance, and perhaps an invitation to a webinar on new product features.

- Include industry news and helpful tips to make your messages interesting and insightful.

- Personalize your communication to the buying role or industry of the prospect:

  - Ask interest and need-related questions on your qualification form and in ongoing nurturing touches, to gain more details about the prospect, and build out your data record.

  - Create landing pages on your website that speak to the specific interests of your targets.

If you are wondering what your B-to-B marketing colleagues are finding most useful in their nurturing programs, look at Table 9.3, which is based on Aberdeen Group research. The nurturing toolkit is a large one, and you can apply it with all the creativity at your disposal.

Table 9.3   Most-Used Content for Nurturing Communications

Nurturing Materials	Usage
Educational materials (white papers, research, and so on)	78%
Webinar invitation	72%
Links to customized landing pages	72%
Product or service information	67%
News and events on the company	44%

Source: Aberdeen Group

WHAT LEAD NURTURING IS NOT

Lead nurturing is not:

- Sending out an occasional e-newsletter.

- Blasting your house file with a new white paper.

- Calling leads every 6 weeks to see if they are ready to buy.

- Offering content that promotes your company's products without regard to the needs or interests of the recipient.

Content Development

The quality of the content you deliver is vital to the success of your lead-nurturing program. Develop a content strategy that begins by assessing your current content assets. What do you have on hand? Develop a detailed inventory of your content assets, organizing them around such variables as:

- Title/name with a unique identifying number or name.

- URL or location where it can be found.

- Medium: Video, PPT, PDF, webinar, eBook, and so on.

- Objective: How-to, case study, testimonial, comparison, research report, and so on.

- Applications: Lead generation, awareness, retention, usage, and so on. (Each piece might have multiple applications, but it's a good idea to organize by the most effective one or two uses.)

- Market segment: Mid-market, large enterprise, consumer, for example.

- Buying role: User, specifier, decision-maker, influencer, gatekeeper, and so on.

- Buying process stage: Need identification, solution identification, vendor selection, purchase, and so on. (This is similar to applications, but another way of looking at it, which can be helpful in campaign planning.)

- Date last updated.

- Freshness indicator: Ready to use? Does it need a refresh?

- Owner or producer within the company.

- Comments/notes.

Then, fill any gaps with appropriate content:

- White papers
- Research reports
- Case studies
- eBooks
- Webinars

Keep in mind that content has a shelf-life. You need to update or replace content regularly, as it ages. Webinars and live event content are the worst culprits—they suffer from a perception of being out of date almost the minute they are over. But a white paper's value can last for years.

Tracking

You won't know how your lead-nurturing program is working without a painstaking tracking process. Tracking also provides you with the data essential to developing relevant messaging in the ongoing nurturing process over time to keep the prospect moving along the buying process.

To develop a robust tracking program, you need to craft your messages with the essential elements of direct response communications:

- Motivational offer or incentive
- A call to action, such as "Click here" or "Call now"
- A response form, such as a landing page or business reply card (BRC) that asks for additional data about prospect needs or interests

As the prospect responds to your messages, set up capture processes for responses through various media, such as:

- Opens
- Clicks
- Links
- Page visits, time spent
- Downloads
- Forwards
- Response time
- Frequency of access
- BRCs received

- Telephone calls attempted, connected, and the disposition
- Voice mail messages left

For more details on response-tracking techniques, see Chapter 10, "Metrics and Tracking."

Triggered Marketing

The ongoing multichannel communications stream required for lead nurturing is very complicated. So it is best executed via triggered marketing techniques that manage the planning and deployment of the streams, by customer segment. Table 9.4 illustrates how an ongoing nurturing stream can be structured and timed to reach the customer over time.

Table 9.4   Sample of a Simple Nurture Contact Flow

Day from Inquiry	Message	Medium
1	Thank you for your inquiry	Phone
7	Research report relevant to request at inquiry	Email
30	Case study of success from company in inquirer's industry	Email
45	Seminar invitation	Phone
60	Customer testimonial and personalized letter	Mail
75	Link to article from trade journal	Email
90	Personal note from sales engineer to schedule online demo	Email
105	White paper and personal cover letter	Mail
125	Invitation to breakfast seminar at trade show	Email

Executing triggered marketing programs can be vastly simplified by the use of one of the new marketing automation systems available today. Sometimes called "drip marketing," these automated systems not only manage the communications, but also route the leads to the appropriate sales resource when they are ready to be worked. Many competing systems are on the market, and some are even optimized for lead-nurturing applications.

When properly applied, campaign-automation tools can make the entire lead-generation process faster and more responsive to customer needs. These tools allow you to:

- Automate lead generation with marketing campaigns across multiple communications channels, such as email and direct mail.
- Gain a detailed view into your lead flow at all stages of the buying process.

- Implement accurate lead scoring to rank leads and identify the right ones to send to the sales team.

- Set up efficient lead nurturing programs to stay in touch with high-potential prospects.

- Analyze campaign ROI at every stage.

Specific to lead nurturing, these platforms enhance the process with tools that:

- Automate the lead follow-up process

- Communicate with prospects based on timeframe, date, response, interest, or behavior

- Continually adjust the lead score based on a combination of activity and response behavior

- Identify newly qualified prospects quickly and route the lead directly to sales via email or CRM integration, for followup.

MARKETING AUTOMATION SYSTEMS

Marketing automation systems designed to assist in the lead nurturing effort are maturing rapidly, adding new useful features, integrating better with other sales and marketing tools, and improving the user interface. New competitors are coming on the scene regularly—and others are being swallowed up in acquisitions and consolidation. Here are some of the current market leaders in the area of lead nurturing; expect plenty of change to this list as the industry evolves:

Eloqua	Marketo
Genius	NurtureHQ
InfusionSoft	Pardot
LeadLife	Silverpop
Manticore Technology	

Making the decision to invest in marketing automation software is a major step for companies large and small. The Aberdeen Group has done some useful research on the value of automation, especially in the lead-nurturing arena. One interesting element of this research is the data on why companies are taking the plunge in the first place (shown in Table 9.5). The top reason for introducing marketing automation is shown to be measurement and tracking.

Table 9.5   The Business Case for Marketing Automation

Reason for Using Lead Management Technology	Respondents
Marketing accountability and measurement	59%
To learn about customers and prospects	50%
Desire to manage multi-channel activities from one application	39%
Inability to prioritize leads for sales	38%

Source: Aberdeen Group

Case Study:
How a Comprehensive Rethinking of Lead Generation and Management Strategy Improved Lead-Nurturing Response Rates and Lowered Costs

Case study (pages 167–173) reprinted with permission of Marketing Sherpa.

Like most marketers, Dave Laverty, vice president of marketing, IBM Cognos, was experiencing changes in the B-to-B lead-generation landscape. Factors such as lengthening sales cycles and expanding buying committees were making traditional tactics less effective at generating demand for the company's business-intelligence software.

Rented email lists weren't performing as well as they used to perform. The company's house email list was being bombarded with offers, and as a result, open and click-through rates were dropping. Laverty and his team needed to work differently.

"A couple years ago, we took on an initiative we called Marketing 2.0," says Laverty. "It was a challenge I gave to our web team to think about how we reach, engage and deliver more information to prospects that could be out there that we hadn't touched yet."

Campaign

The team's Marketing 2.0 initiative examined their marketing strategy in the context of three major goals:

- Presenting the company as a thought-leader
- Generating demand
- Supporting and enabling the sales team

They saw a lead-nurturing strategy as the common thread connecting those three goals and developed a new process to shape outreach efforts, engage prospects, and qualify them for the sales team.

Here are four key strategies they used to refine their lead-nurturing process:

Strategy #1. Revamp website with additional offers.

Laverty and his team first examined how well their website functioned as an entry point into the lead-nurturing funnel.

"We looked at [our website] as a demand-generating tool," says Laverty. "We have a lot of people passing by our window, so to speak. What are we doing to encourage those people to come in, browse and engage with us?"

With engagement in mind, the team overhauled its website to provide additional offers and features for prospects. Their goal was to appeal to a wide range of prospects and to determine which types of offers or content strategies created the most interest.

The result was a site that included:

- Varying types of content, such as white papers, online demos, events, and online communities.
- Information organized by product line or business task, such as performance management, budgeting and forecasting, measurement and reporting, and score-carding.
- Information organized by industry, such as finance, government, retail, manufacturing, and health care.

Prospects who wanted to download content or register for events were required to fill out a web form. That form helped establish a prospect profile.

Key fields included:

- Name
- Company
- Industry
- Department
- Job title

Strategy #2. Create a lead-nurturing program based on prospect profile.

The website served as the entry point for the team's new lead-nurturing program, which sent additional relevant offers based on the prospect's profile and previous activity. See Figure 9.1 for a visual depiction of the nurturing process.

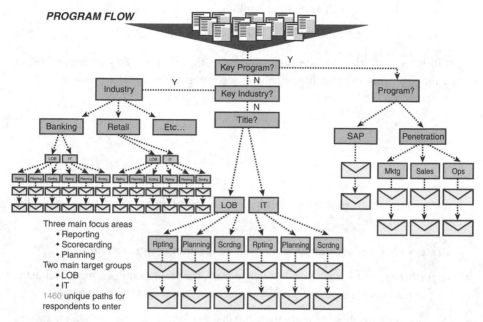

Figure 9.1   Lead nurturing process flowchart.

Information from registration forms was sent back to the team's central data warehouse. There, the data was analyzed for variables, such as:

- New or returning prospect
- Frequency of visits
- Additional contact within customer company
- Previous actions taken

Each prospect then received an initial follow-up response that was relevant to the offer to which they had responded. For example, if a prospect viewed an online demo on reporting, they would receive a follow-up offer for a reporting white paper.

Two more follow-up emails pointed prospects to additional relevant content, and invited prospects to contact a member of the sales team, or sign up for an email newsletter.

The follow-up touches were automated to deliver a flow of offers based on three major categories:

- Key marketing program, such as promotions around an annual event, a product launch, or a campaign aimed at prospects using SAP or other software

- Key industry, such as retail or banking
- Job title targets, such as IT or line-of-business managers

Within each of those three primary categories, the team created a custom sequence of messages that were further organized according to three major product focus areas:

- Reporting
- Score-carding
- Planning

The result of that segmentation strategy was 1,460 unique lead nurturing paths for prospects to enter.

Strategy #3. Conduct statistical analysis of marketing interactions.

To further refine their lead nurturing program, the team examined historical data for correlations among variables in the marketing cycle and their outcomes.

Working off a database of more than 200,000 marketing interactions, the team conducted a statistical analysis to help them prioritize their marketing tactics and investments.

Trends uncovered during this analysis included:

- Online demos had the highest rate of opportunity creation.
- Face-to-face events had the largest impact on increasing deal size and close rate.
- The conversion rate from lead-to-opportunity virtually died 10 days after the prospect first engaged with an offer or piece of content.

"We were finally getting some definitive answers to those questions about response rate and types of offer to provide," says Laverty. "We saw that the faster we can get someone in front of an online demo, that has the highest success rate for opportunity creation."

Strategy #4. Test response time for the three-touch nurturing program.

Statistical analysis gave the team a new hypothesis to test with their automated three-touch email protocol.

Historical data indicated higher lead-to-opportunity conversion rates when prospects had repeated interactions with the company within 24 hours of registration. So, the team decided to condense the time between its automated response emails.

The tested the following nurturing schedules:

- First response email (see Figure 9.2 for a sample): 2 days versus 4 hours after registration

Figure 9.2   The first response email, sent four hours after registration.

- Second response email (see Figure 9.3): 10 days versus 24 hours later
- Third response email (see Figure 9.4): 20 days versus 10 days later

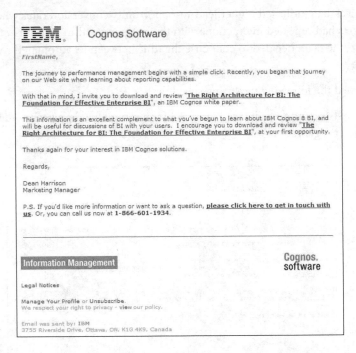

Figure 9.3   The second response email, sent 24 hours after registration.

Figure 9.4   The third response email, sent 10 days after registration.

Results

The team's adoption and refinement of its lead-nurturing strategy yielded dramatic results.

Thanks to the new website, roughly 11 percent of website visitors now complete a registration form. That compares to an average industry capture rate of 3 percent.

The team compared results from its segmented, three-touch nurturing emails to those of traditional multi-touch campaigns to the entire house list. The improvement was remarkable:

- Open rates increased from 13.2 percent to 33.3 percent

- Click-through rates increased from 0.09 percent to 15.5 percent

- Response rate increased from 0.05 percent to 17.5 percent

The team has reduced its cost-per-lead 30–40 percent.

Better alignment between sales and marketing goals means that Laverty's team generates 30% of the company's pipeline per quarter.

"We've been able to hold our investments relatively flat, as well as increase our productivity," says Laverty. "I would say that's a pretty big contributor to marketing having a seat at the table."

Laverty notes that the changes reflect an ongoing process that's not yet complete. Their approach requires a series of smaller steps and tests, which can then be rolled out across the enterprise.

For example, the team adopted shortened response times for their three-touch nurturing program after testing it against their standard schedule.

The four-hour/24-hour/10-day schedule achieved:

- A 100 percent increase in open rate, compared to the company average.

- A 1,600 percent increase in CTR, compared to the company average.

"It's a combination of all these things—having the data in place, the systems in place to execute, and then staying on top of the data—that's turning our marketing efforts into a science."

Reprinted with permission of Marketing Sherpa

10

Metrics and Tracking

Metrics matter in every business. These days, every pro-fessional must prove results with quantification. This is nothing new for experienced lead-generation marketers. Measurement is at the heart of the process in response rate percentages, cost per lead, and ROI. But measured reporting specifically on marketing performance can be tough, to say the least. What are you measuring when considering lead-generation campaign productivity? Market share? Response rate? Purchase intent? Lead volume or quality? Sales?

If measurement is tough for marketers in general, it's even tougher for business-to-business (B-to-B) marketers, because of:

- The complexity of the sale, which involves multiple parties, each of which has an impact on results.

- The length of the sales cycle, which requires campaigns that use a series of touches over time.

- Flawed reporting on lead-closure results from your sales team, or completely unavailable sales figures from partners or resellers.

- Multiple touches through different media, which make it impossible to tell which one clinched the sale or which, if any, could have been done without.

Rather than tearing your hair out in the face of this complexity, the best approach is to narrow your focus in lead-generation measurement to five essential metrics: response rate, cost per lead, inquiry-to-lead conversation rate, lead-to-sales conversion rate, and expense-to-revenue ratio (E:R). These are discussed in the first part of this chapter.

Response Rate

The problem with response rate isn't so much capturing responses and calculating the rate. You can do that for any given outbound communication by using a key code, a unique landing page, a pixel, or an 800 number to connect the inbound response with the original outbound message. Any communication that asks for a response can be measured this way.

However, there are problems stemming from the general complexity of a typical lead-generation program. There are a multitude of variables that drive campaign results—the target list, the offer, the creative, to name a few. Just knowing the response rate to a specific campaign touch doesn't tell you much about the campaign's effectiveness or how to fix it if it's ineffective. Only a controlled test will give you those answers. In short, as a measure of effective marketing, response rate, well—doesn't rate.

For most campaign analysis purposes, a more useful metric is cost per inquiry. For the record, however, there are helpful industry benchmarks on response rates, thanks to years of tracking by the Direct Marketing Association (DMA), which publishes its *Response Rate Trend Report* regularly. So you can compare the response rates of your campaign elements to these industry standards, and draw conclusions on whether you are in the ball park or not. Tables 10.1 through 10.9 show some of the most recent stats, culled from the 2010 study. Let's look at each in more detail.

Tables 10.1 and 10.2 show response rates reported for lead-generation campaigns using mail and direct mail, to names on house files (typically customers and inquirers) versus names from prospect files (usually lists rented from outside list owners). These numbers do not break out business from consumer lead-generation programs, but likely most of the survey responders were reporting on B-to-B situations.

Table 10.1   Email Metrics for Lead Generation

	House File	Prospect File
Open rate	24.57%	12.28%
Click-through rate	6.67%	3.31%
Conversion rate	1.94%	.65%
Bounce rate	3.84%	5.04%
Unsubscribe rate	.74%	1.66%

Source: The DMA 2010 Response Rate Report

Table 10.2   Direct Mail Metrics for Lead Generation

Format	House File Response Rate	Prospect File Response Rate	Cost Per Lead
Letter-size envelope	4.74%	1.8%	$82.53
Postcard	5.23%	2.17%	$98.74
Oversized envelope	4.37%	1.61%	$230.69
Dimensional	8%	4.82%	$197.26

Source: The DMA 2010 Response Rate Report

Tables 10.3, 10.4, and 10.5 display reported results for lead-generation campaigns using paid search engine marketing (SEM), banner advertising, and outbound telemarketing. These results combine both house and prospect file targets.

Table 10.3   Paid Search Metrics for Lead Generation

Metric	Result
Cost per click	$1.83
Conversion rate	5.92%

Source: The DMA 2010 Response Rate Report

Table 10.4   Display (Banner) Advertising for Lead Generation

Metric	Result
CPM (cost per thousand)	$15.23
CPA (cost per action)	$35.83
CTR (click-through rate)	80%
Conversion rate	5.69%

Source: The DMA 2010 Response Rate Report

Table 10.5   Outbound Telemarketing for Lead Generation

Objective	Response Rate	Cost Per Contact
Cross-sell/upsell	14.28%	$10
Prospecting	9.48%	$16.01

Source: The DMA 2010 Response Rate Report

The DMA Response Rate Report also presented data on campaign results by industry. Tables 10.6 and 10.7 show the results for house file and prospecting mail and email in the technology and manufacturing sectors, and Tables 10.8 and 10.9 show benchmarks in the business services sector. In technology and manufacturing, 50 percent of respondents said they use direct mail, and 59 percent said they use email. In business services, 67 percent of respondents claimed to use each medium.

Table 10.6   Direct Mail Response Rate Benchmarks for Technology and Manufacturing

Format	House File Response Rate	Prospect File Response Rate	Cost Per Lead
Letter-size envelope	11.45%	3%	$13.36
Postcard	7.87%	2.29%	NA
Dimensional	12%	7.75%	NA

Source: The DMA 2010 Response Rate Report

Table 10.7   Email Response Rate Benchmarks for Technology and Manufacturing

	House File	Prospect File
Open rate	14.18%	8.12%
Click-through rate	9.62%	3.63%
Conversion rate	5.32%	.13%
Bounce rate	2.15%	4.23%
Unsubscribe rate	.64%	1.52%

Source: The DMA 2010 Response Rate Report

Table 10.8   Direct Mail Response Rate Benchmarks for Business Services

Format	House File Response Rate	Prospect File Response Rate	Cost Per Lead
Letter-size envelope	3.41%	1.78%	$323.75
Postcard	4.54%	2.01%	$44.88
Oversized envelope	2.83%	1.78%	$38.92

Source: The DMA 2010 Response Rate Report

Table 10.9   Email Response Rate Benchmarks for Business Services

	House File	Prospect File
Open rate	29.25%	15.17%
Click-through rate	10.85%	3.44%
Conversion rate	2.95%	1.47%
Bounce rate	6.89%	7.97%
Unsubscribe rate	1.21%	1.46%

Source: The DMA 2010 Response Rate Report

Cost Per Lead

Most third graders have the math background to figure out cost per lead: Divide the amount the campaign cost by the number of leads the campaign produced. But there is some judgment involved. For one thing, you must decide which number to

use as the denominator: the total number of inquiries produced or only the qualified leads.

There are arguments on both sides. One can maintain that in B-to-B lead generation, the true test of a marketing campaign's worth is its capability to provide the
sales organization with *qualified* leads—the ones that improve sales force productivity, reduce cold calling, and increase the amount of time sales people can spend in
front of their hottest prospects.

One can also maintain that knowing how many prospects in total expressed interest
is indeed meaningful, as it provides a broad picture of the "front end."

The truth is, either approach is valid. So are both. So it is recommended that you
capture both cost per inquiry and cost per qualified lead. You'll gain the most intelligence and largest number of options going forward. If you choose only one, be
sure to stick with it over time so you can compare campaigns on an apples-to-
apples basis.

One more issue needs to be addressed when calculating this important metric—the
cost elements that are gathered up to comprise the numerator. Most experienced
direct marketing professionals argue that only variable campaign costs should be in
the numerator. This includes items such as list expense, outside creative development by agencies and freelancers, and an estimate of variable expense for inquiry
handling and the cost of fulfilling any premium or download. Calculating these
costs can be a challenge when, for example, a white paper is created for one campaign but used for a variety of purposes. You might want to get help from an internal cost accountant to develop rules for such situations.

The greater issue is what you do about the fixed costs involved in lead-generation
campaigns—that is, items such as marketing staff salaries, in-house agency and call
center infrastructure, and other expenses that might have multiple applications
beyond lead generation and management. Here, too, it's a good idea to sit with a
finance professional to work these matters out. In medium to large companies, most
lead-generation programs are costed based on variable expense, but in smaller companies, there might be good reason to include fixed expenses in the numerator. No
matter how you determine what goes into lead-generation costs, be sure you use the
same methodology across campaigns and over time, so your results can be compared correctly.

THERE'S ALWAYS ROOM FOR MORE METRICS

Hugh McFarlane, author of *The Leaky Funnel*, identifies additional metrics that marketing should consider tracking. These kick in after the lead has been passed to sales, and they provide more insight into the lead's capability to drive revenue:

- **Sales qualified leads (SQLs).** The percent of the leads the sales organization is willing to accept and work on. Despite marketing's best effort to ensure a lead is qualified before passing it on, sales will always reject some. A typical reason: "We are already in that account."

- **First meetings.** The percentage of sales-qualified leads that resulted in a meeting or a similar concrete action.

- **Proposals.** Sales needs to make an offer that can be accepted or rejected. What percent of your first meetings resulted in some sort of proposal being made?

- **Closed deals.** The percentage of sales offers accepted or closed.

Inquiry-to-Lead Conversion Rate

The rate by which inquiries convert to qualified leads depends on two factors: the quality of the inquiry and the preciseness of the qualification criteria. If marketing and sales have developed the qualification questions together, the second factor should remain pretty consistent over time (although you might need to tweak the criteria for various products and audiences). However, the quality of the inquiries is a different story. So many variables can have an impact—the medium, the timing, the list, the offer, the creative. Think of the conversion rate as an early warning signal that campaign refinements might be needed to improve the quality of the inquiry. The most likely culprit is a too-generous offer. Another possibility is that you might use media that attracts the less committed.

The inquiry-to lead-conversion rate can be seen within the context of a variety of "activity-based" metrics that live in the sole purview of the marketing function. Activity-based lead-generation campaign metrics include:

Cost per thousand

Response rate

Cost per inquiry

Campaign turn-around time

Qualification rate (inquiry-to-lead conversion)

Cost per qualified lead

Following activity-based metrics enables the marketing function to compare campaign results across campaigns, and over time, creating a benchmark for measuring continuous improvement. The beauty of this type of metric is that it avoids the vexing problems arising from trying to capture sales results and attaching them to specific campaign activity. However, for delivering value to the company and its owners, results-based metrics paint a far stronger picture of a lead-generation campaign's value.

METRICS BY PROXY: GET A SNEAK PEEK AT RESULTS

Business-to-business marketers are nothing if not patient. Because of the long B-to-B sales cycles, a campaign's revenue pay-off can take months or years. But what if you need to assess campaign productivity before the sales cycle has ended? Consider applying "proxy" metrics to your campaign results. Robert Reneau of National Semiconductor assigns an estimated dollar value to each interim campaign outcome instead of waiting for a sale. If a customer downloads a piece of content, for example, the campaign is credited with $1,000. A product sample request is worth $5,000, and a lead entered into the sales force automation system "earns" $50,000. Can seemingly arbitrary numbers correlate with actual sales results? Over time, National says they do. This sneak peek allows managers not only early comparison of campaign productivity by product or by business unit, but lets them step in and make mid-course corrections if needed.

Lead-to-Sales Conversion Rates

No surprise, the lead-to-sales conversion rate is calculated by dividing the number of qualified campaign leads (which were handed off to sales) by the number of leads that eventually result in a sale. This metric can range broadly, from as little as 5 percent to as high as 50 percent, generally as a factor of lead quality, sales skill, and—truth be told—the capability of your processes to match a sale to a lead in the first place. In many companies, especially those using third-party distribution channels, this is not an easy task. Some methods for getting around the problem are discussed later in this chapter.

Like most metrics, the lead-to-sales conversion rate is best applied over time, to compare campaign to campaign, offer to offer, or channel to channel. If the lead-to-sales rate declines or disappoints, where should the fault-finding finger point? Did sales fall down on the job? Did marketing deliver inferior leads? This metric can shed some light on this age-old debate. Keep an eye on this conversion rate over time by marketing campaign, by rep (or groups of reps), by sales channel, and any other variable that might be ready for some fine tuning.

The lead-to-sales conversion rate can be viewed in the context of a variety of "results-based" metrics, which depend on sales results to be assessed. As mentioned previously, results-based metrics are preferable, wherever possible, because they get closer to an explanation of whether the marketing campaign actually paid off financially. But these metrics are problematic for many B-to-B lead-generation marketers, because sales cycles are so long, and sales people are less than motivated to report to marketing on how any given lead really performed. So it can be difficult to connect an actual closed deal to a specific lead that might have been involved.

When sales results can be assessed, the most useful metrics then become:

Conversion-to-sales rate

Sales revenue per lead

Campaign ROI

Campaign expense-to-revenue ratio

Expense-to-Revenue Ratio (E:R)

Traditionally, marketers use ROI as the definitive metric for campaign effectiveness. However, in business marketing, ROI is problematic, in a highly unusual way: Campaign ROIs are often so big they look ridiculous. It's entirely within the realm of possibility, as shown in Table 10.10, to spend $30,000 on a campaign that eventually generates $3.6 million in sales, producing a campaign ROI of 11,900 percent.

This happens because business revenues are often large compared to marketing expenses, and the lead-generation campaign is often a tiny part of the total cost of sales. The true ROI on a program needs to take into account the direct costs of both sales and marketing. To measure marketing's contribution, it's often better to calculate the expense-to-revenue ratio (E:R) instead. In the $30,000 / 3.6 million example, as also shown in Table 10.10, this works out to be a respectable—and credible—3.75%.

Table 10.10   Comparing E:R with Campaign ROI

Campaign Element	Assumptions and Calculations
Campaign expense	$30,000
Qualified leads generated	200
Cost per qualified lead ($30,000 / 200)	$150
Lead-to-sales conversion rate	40%
Leads converting to sales (200 * .40)	80
Average order size (or average incremental revenue)	$100,000
Cost per sale ($30,000 / 80)	$375
Sales revenue (80 * $100,000)	$8 million
Gross margin rate	45%
Gross margin on the campaign revenue ($8 million * .45)	$3.6 million
E:R ($30,000 / $8 million)	3.75%
ROI ([$3.6 million − $30,000] / $30,000)	11,900%

MEASUREMENT RULES! GOOD ADVICE FOR PLANNING YOUR METRICS

When choosing the two or three metrics by which you will assess campaign value year after year, keep in mind the following tips from the experts:

- **Keep measurements simple and relevant.** Richard Vancil of the research company IDC and chair of a conference on B-to-B metrics sponsored by his company, maintains that the larger your company, the simpler your performance measures should be. Only metrics specific to your business situation should be employed. Yahoo!, for example, no longer tracks awareness metrics for its brand. Everyone knows the brand by now.

- **Monitor your pipeline.** Marketers concern should not be limited to the quantity and quality of the leads distributed to sales. You need to keep an eye on the entire marketing pipeline. Gottfried Sehringer, vice president of marketing at Softrax, instituted such a management system and learned some surprising facts: 43 percent of his campaign responses comprised duplicate contacts within target accounts, and only 2.5 percent of gross campaign responses converted to qualified leads ready for the sales team.

- **Budget for it.** If your most important metrics include anything other than sales leads, prepare to spend money gathering the data. Valerie Mason Cunningham, vice president of corporate marketing services at Xerox, said she spends 50 percent of her resources on tracking fuzzy marketing investments such as sponsorships and "brand esteem" among her target audience segments.

Seven Techniques for Tracking Leads to Closure

Tracking goes hand in hand with measurement as an essential element of sound B-to-B management. You need to know what happens after a lead is generated by a campaign. Was it followed up? Converted to a sale? Lost to the competition? Returned for further nurturing? You need feedback, but sales teams are not renowned for their conscientious reporting. Besides, you don't want to divert too much of their time and energy away from selling.

If sales has lead-tracking software available, your chances of receiving timely information will be better. If not, keep the reporting system simple and convenient and be persistent if reports are delayed.

In a complex, multitouch campaign, where a lead may take months, even more than a year, to close, and where third-party distributors or channel partners may be involved, it can be difficult to connect a campaign lead to an actual piece of closed revenue. But with some care, you ought to be able to make the connection by using one or more of the following techniques. Each of these seven tracking techniques has benefits and limitations. Weigh the pros and cons as you consider using one or several in tandem.

The Whole Story: A Closed-Loop System

A closed-loop system is a process, often enabled by special software, that tries to track each qualified lead to its end sales result: sale, no sale, or loss of the sale to the competition. Many sales force automation (SFA) systems include lead tracking as part of their functionality.

In effect, the closed-loop system allows marketing to feed a lead to the appropriate sales rep, and the sales team then reports on where the lead is in its selling process, by key entering the status of the lead as it moves along. A typical lead-management process on the sales side begins with the assigned sales person accepting the lead, at which point it might be called an "opportunity. Then, the sales person may further qualify it (whereby it becomes a sales-qualified lead versus its prior status as a marketing-qualified lead). Sales might indicate that the lead is "open," meaning it has not been contacted yet, or "working," meaning that the sales person is in touch with the prospect. Additional stages might include a forecast of likelihood to convert and the eventual close. Companies might set up their sales process stages differently, but in any case, the closed-loop system relies on self-reporting by sales people.

If you decide to put this kind of system into place, plan to spend lots of time asking the sales force for information—but don't plan on obtaining that information easily. Sales people are busy, and they want and need to stay focused on selling. You should also plan to spend some money, because closed-loop software systems are expensive. They are most applicable with high-value products and services.

Some marketers find that the closed-loop system under-reports results, because the sales force might not be sufficiently motivated to do the required key entry. Another frequent problem is that a sales person might be tempted to change the source code on a lead, which has the effect of denying credit for it to the marketing department altogether. In such situations, you have two options: You can go back and identify leads that were not properly tracked through the system—a time-consuming process—or you can supplement your closed-loop system with other techniques, which are discussed in the following sections.

Buyers Tell All: End-User Sampling

This inexpensive, reliable technique is based on surveys to a statistically projectable sample of end users who were promoted in a particular campaign. It is also particularly useful for capturing actual sales from multiple channels.

Here's how it works. Pull a sample from one of two sources: either prospects who were contacted in the outbound campaign or inquiries who responded to the campaign. Wait a reasonable period after the campaign, a period about the length of your typical sales cycle. Survey your sample by phone, email, or mail, strictly limiting questions to the purchase itself. Ask if they bought the product and where they bought it; and if they didn't buy it, ask if they solved their business problem some other way or purchased from the competition. If they purchased from a distributor, you might also want to ask how much they paid for the product.

Discipline yourself to keep your survey questions only to matters of the purchase. Do not ask if they received the campaign message. This is not market research to help you improve the campaign or gain customer insights. If you confuse the end-user sampling survey with classic market research, your survey will lengthen, reducing its focus and—worse—lowering its response rate.

After your sampling results are in, you will have clear data on what percentage of campaign contacts actually bought. By projecting the sample to the whole, you should be able to make a reasonable assessment of the sales results from the campaign. Invariably, you will uncover accounts that did make a purchase, but the sale was not captured by your closed-loop tracking system, if you have one. That means you will have more legitimate, documentable campaign revenue to claim for marketing.

End-user sampling is particularly effective when a third-party distribution channel sits between you and the customer. Often, distributors feel that they "own" the relationship with the end customer, and they are legitimately hesitant—or outright unwilling—to share sales results with the company for which they are distributing. The end-user sampling method provides a neat way to circumvent that problem and get actual data on customer buying. Just keep in mind: You must take care not to over-survey customers or they will get annoyed.

By All Accounts: Data Match-Back

Data match-back is an excellent, low-cost way to track closed revenue to campaigns. It works only when you have direct access to the account that made the purchase. If a distributor sells the product for you, you might not have visibility into which company bought—unless you have a systems where the distributor does the selling but you deliver or bill the account.

To employ this technique, wait after a campaign for the average length of a sales cycle, similar to the end-user sampling method previously. Then, compare the accounts that received the campaign to the accounts that purchased the promoted product. In effect, you are "matching back" the purchase to the campaign, and crediting the campaign for at least part of the buying decision. It's best to do this match-back at the site level versus the contact level, because the person you contacted in the campaign is just as likely not to be the person who actually placed the order.

Politically speaking, match-back can be a bit dangerous. A lead-generation campaign has—one hopes—plenty of influence on generating sales. But marketing should avoid claiming full credit for all the sales in any given account—even the sales of a particular product in a particular account that was promoted in a campaign. This is because there are plenty of positive influences on any B-to-B sale—the attentions from field and inside sales, messaging from corporate communications, word of mouth from satisfied customers, the lead-generation campaign and other influences. So, a wise marketer uses match-back data to show that the campaign had some role to play in the sales at a site—call it an "assist," perhaps. But it is best to avoid taking credit for all the sales indicated by data match-back.

Isolation Ward: Control Groups

A control group technique selects a certain set of customers and suppresses them from promotion in a campaign. Later, sales in the control accounts are compared to sales in the accounts that received the campaign. The lift in revenue associated with accounts receiving the campaign can then be attributed to the campaign itself.

In theory, establishing a control group for every campaign is a scientifically provable way to assess campaign results. In practice, however, control groups are just about impossible to implement in the broader world of business marketing. Because a control group isolates a set of customers who won't see the campaign, and compares sales in these accounts versus a set of similar accounts who were promoted, control groups in effect leave money on the table. The more the campaign is shown to be effective in driving revenue, the more money is lost by nonpromotion to the control group. It's a rare management team, not to mention shareholder, who will cotton to suppressing from promotions certain accounts that are likely to generate revenue.

However, control groups can come in handy in certain situations. In a multitouch campaign, for example, control groups and test groups can be set up to let you determine the ideal sequence or number of touches.

For Your Eyes Only: Exclusive Offers

The logic behind this strategy is indisputable: When you can create an offer that is promoted only in a particular campaign, every sale using that offer can be reliably attributed to that campaign. In the same fashion, coupons or special offers redeemable through distribution channels but funded by the marketer allow reliable tracking of campaign results.

The problem with exclusive offers, however, is that they are difficult to scale. You need to come up with a new offer for each campaign. Or, you have to repeat the offer only after a considerable time has passed, so the waters are not muddied by overlapping use of the offer. For best results, use exclusive offers in single tactic campaigns for products with short sales cycles.

Sign Me Up: Product Registration

Product registration has been used successfully by technology marketers for decades, and the method has the benefit of not only building a customer relationship over time, but also serving as a way to identify the connection of a sale to a marketing effort. On the face of it, product registration would seem to be the ultimate end-user sampling technique: When the customer registers the product, he or she indicates where or when the purchase was made and answers other questions, such as what influenced the purchase decision. The thorny part is linking registration questions back to specific campaigns without a barrage of tiresome, off-putting questions, which likely reduce registration rates.

End with the Handoff: Activity-Based Measurements

When other techniques are too expensive or too problematic to justify, you may opt to measure only your lead-generation activities—those occurring before the handoff to sales, such as response rate, conversion rate to qualified lead, cost per lead, campaign executed on time, on budget, and others. This approach is not recommended because it fails to connect lead-generation programs to tangible sales results, demonstrating a clear return on investment. But in some situations, relying strictly on the activities strictly under marketing control can make sense. If your lead-generation programs are designed to support a distribution partner channel, for example, where the terms of the partner relationship require lead generation but do not require any lead tracking or results reporting, activity-based measurement is the way to go.

WHO GETS THE CREDIT?

No one is ever happy in business-to-business. If a lead is generated from a website and closed by a face-to-face field rep, who gets credit for the sale? Of course, the sales person deserves a commission, no matter where the business originates. The field team deserves to credit the sale against its channel quota. But what about the lead-generation marketing team? Don't they deserve some credit? And what about the fulfillers, the qualifiers, and the nurturers? If their salaries are supplemented with performance-based bonuses, they will certainly want a piece of the action.

Crediting the sale to the parties involved is, in effect, the flip side of the problem of assigning marketing costs to the various parties. It isn't easy, but it's worth coming up with some kind of agreement that reduces squabbling and allows a modicum of peace in the land. Many companies solve the problem by double counting, for internal purposes, allowing each group that touched the process to make some claim on the revenue—and take some hit for the expense.

When a Lead Doesn't Close

The sad truth is that not all leads close. After a reasonable amount of time, if a lead does not convert to a sale it should come back to marketing. What next? Here are some options:

- **Hand it off to another sales rep.** A new approach may work.

- **Hang it up.** The prospect may no longer be ready to buy. Give the lead a rest.

- **Reclassify and requalify.** Consider it an inquiry and put it through the qualification process again.

- **Reclassify and store.** Consider it a prospect and put it back in the marketing database.

You should track how each situation performs, so you can continue to refine your approach and streamline your system.

11

The Fast-Evolving Future of Lead Generation

In the past ten years, lead generation has changed dramatically, driven heavily by the availability of the Internet and its influence on how business buyers behave. The changes show no sign of slowing down. It seems like every day exciting new developments come along to change and grow our ability to generate high-quality leads.

In this chapter, I make some predictions about what's on the horizon. Here are ten developments that we are likely to see.

1. More and Better Marketing Automation

The forward-thinking B-to-B marketing consultancy SiriusDecisions estimates that, while only 8–12 percent of B-to-B marketing organizations had installed a marketing automation platform as of 2010, that percentage will rise to 50 percent by 2015. The consultancy also identifies several important developments in marketing automation functionality that are likely to come on the scene, making our lead-generation lives easier. These include the following:

- Integration with social media monitoring tools

- Support for multiple concurrent scoring methods, which will allow such sophisticated analysis as measuring a single customer's interest in multiple products

- More powerful predictive capabilities

New ancillary tools will emerge, too. As Jim Obermayer, founder of the Sales Lead Management Association, points out, such tools as Nimble and Shade Tree Technology already facilitate access to a variety of social media and databases, providing virtually instant access to information about people and companies within customer relationship management (CRM) applications.

2. Sales and Marketing Will Finally Get on the Same Page

Jim Obermayer predicts that marketing automation is destined to merge with sales force automation altogether. Oracle's purchase of Market2Lead is an early example of this expected trend. I fervently hope the trend continues, because it would be one excellent, effective way to bridge the chasm in understanding that has historically kept these groups apart, taking potshots at each other across the divide. With an increasingly Internet-informed prospect base, it's more important than ever to stop the squabbling and team up to develop effective new strategies.

Marketing can step up by getting well informed about the contents of the sales plan and bringing the sales team in at every stage of the marketing process to gain its buy-in and better understand its needs and goals. Here are some other tips for playing well with sales: Ask for their help in defining the criteria for lead qualification and deliver only leads that meet those standards. Even if you have a fantastic closed-loop lead-tracking system, bite your tongue before bragging that your marketing program drove the sale. Limit yourself to activity-based measures, such as cost-per-qualified lead, and let sales claim the revenues.

3. New Data Sources for Prospecting

It seems like new sources of prospect information arrive on a regular basis. Of great value to the lead-generation prospecting effort in recent years have been Internet-fueled databases, such as Jigsaw and ZoomInfo. So, it's likely that eager entrepreneurs will hit on additional ideas in the future to help us find new prospective buyers more easily or cheaply—or both. As an example, have a look at Cardbrowser.com, which shows signs of promise as a possible new data source. Cardbrowser gathers scads of business cards from exhibitors at trade shows in the high-tech world, scans and duplicates them, and makes them available for download in spreadsheet format. Interesting.

4. Social Media Will Get Real for Lead Generation

Social media is tantalizingly attractive for B-to-B marketers, but hard to pin down for predictable, ongoing lead-generation campaign work. Today, it acts more like PR—exciting, buzz-generating, great for building awareness, and even inquiries, but hard to count on when you have to meet a quota.

My prediction is that someone will eventually—finally—figure out how to convert social media to a reliable lead-generation tool. I'm not sure how this will happen, but these new media channels are too big, with too much potential, to fail us.

While I am at it, I also predict that new social media channels and platforms will continue to emerge to add to the mix. We are so lucky to be alive in these exciting times.

Let's get some insights from Jan Wallen, my colleague who literally "wrote the book" on LinkedIn, *Mastering LinkedIn in 7 Days or Less.* Jan has a well-informed opinion about how social media is going to evolve to serve lead-generation purposes:

> "LinkedIn is already an important resource for lead qualification. With social media, and especially with LinkedIn—which just reached 100 million members—we have accurate information at our fingertips. We can now search for people in our target audience and decision-makers with the same criteria that we used to use for mailing lists.

> "For example, I recently did a search on LinkedIn for CEOs of information technology companies in one New York City zip code. There were more than 3,000 of them! I can look at their LinkedIn profiles to confirm that they are a decision maker for my products and services. I have accurate information on who is in that position, and I know something

about them from their LinkedIn profile before we contact them or decide to market to them. This isn't the same as qualifying them, but it's a better starting point than if we have only a company name. I can also do a company search on LinkedIn to find out how I am already connected with people within that company. Then I can leverage the relationships I already have to get introductions into a company (a new account, for example) or to the specific decision maker I want to target.

"I believe that social media will continue to expand and enhance our generation of quality leads that are more likely to turn into business."

I think Jan is right.

5. Affinity Marketing Will Come to B-to-B

The idea of affinity marketing coming to B-to-B comes from my colleague Denise Olivares, a seasoned financial services marketer, who has seen some early signs of business marketers sharing membership and customer lists with carefully selected partners for mutual benefit. For the same reasons that have hampered the development of B-to-B mailing list rental, it's unlikely that affinity marketing will ever reach consumer levels. But, when two organizations' interests align, the resulting alliance can be a promising prospecting resource. Denise elaborates:

"I think there may be a resurgence in developing affinity relationships in B-to-B. Membership organizations and businesses with reliable data and current information will make themselves available in ever more affinity relationship marketing efforts. I don't mean to say there will be widespread selling of lists, because the market probably would not tolerate that. However, selectively, organizations will be able to sell lists, or more likely, will be charged by their members in finding meaningful partnerships through which they can bring value to the members."

6. Face-to-Face Events Will Resume Their Importance

Trade shows and proprietary corporate events have taken a beating in recent years, it's true. But their value in B-to-B—despite threats like the rise of virtual trade shows and reduced travel budgets—will continue to make them an important and efficient part of the marketing toolkit.

I was impressed by a comment made recently by my colleague Mary Brandon, VP of Marketing at SoftServe, Inc., who said, "I am finding out more and more, both last year and this, that face-to-face events are bringing in the best lead-to-sales conversion rates. I have increased my events budget, and the return on investment has been fantastic. I have our sales and market teams as attendees, speakers, and exhibitors at industry events, CIO round tables, and one-on-one conferences. I have created a series of half-day workshops held throughout the U.S. on our company's expertise such as cloud computing, mobility, new software development trends, and so on. In my 30-year career in marketing, I have discovered that what works well for one company does not work well for all companies. However, I have never seen where face-to-face encounters don't turn out to be a great source for leads."

7. New Ways to Nurture

Is it just pride or wishful thinking to predict that we're all going to continue to get better at marketing? It's probably a bit of both. But, I am convinced that in the area of nurturing, the field is wide open for innovation and improvement. As an example, consider this point from my colleague Stephen D. Armstrong, principal at The 360 Marketer:

> "One trend I have seen emerge is the use of personalized web portals for drip marketing to prospects over an extended sales cycle. My experience has been with health care information technology, like electronic medical records and clinical information systems, which can take 9–18 months to close for the usual reasons, like complex evaluation criteria, multiple stakeholders, high ticket, etc. These portals become a way to maintain a conversation and nurture the relationship by selecting content that is relevant to their lead status and particular issues. With a personalized portal, the seller can track the prospect's engagement via metrics such as portal access, which documents were viewed, and follow-up contacts. It also presents the vendor in a technology-forward light."

According to Armstrong, here's how the process works in a shared portal environment: "Once contact has been established and there is a sense that there is a mutual interest in continuing a conversation, we would create the portal—with no incremental cost, configured from a template, and populated with some initial content—and then we invite them to go to the portal via an email. The copy in the invitation conveys the benefit of engaging together within the portal. This message is also conveyed in direct conversation with the prospect. Each time new content is added, the prospect receives an email alerting them that Company XYZ has just added fresh information, which keeps the company and the shared portal top of mind and prompts return visits.

"This technology has the added benefit of promoting collaboration on lead nurturing between sales and marketing. Marketing would create the portals and be responsible for content population. Sales would be members of the portal, too. Either marketing or sales could continue to drip-market to the prospects, but typically marketing handles content and sales addresses questions posted by the customer and evaluates client interest via the level of their portal activity."

Sounds like a great system.

8. Ever-Evolving Customer Behavior

We've all observed that business buyers are just consumers in company clothing. But, the pace of change is accelerating. Their business-buying behavior is getting more and more like their consumer behavior. Jim Obermayer points out that business buyers already expect fast turnaround, and they are likely to demand almost instantaneous responses from manufacturers they visit on the Internet. We have to keep up!

9. More and Better Video

Video is just now beginning to reach its potential in B-to-B marketing. The trend is definitely upward. Beyond today's basics, with video testimonials and demos, we'll see more applications of video in the marketing toolkit, such as case studies, white papers, advance presentations of new product, and more. One big reason? The disappearing boundary between business buyer and consumer behavior. Watching videos is firmly entrenched in people's daily routines. According to a 2010 survey published by video ad company YuMe, 49 percent of respondents watch videos online every day, and 48 percent expect to watch more online videos in the future. Smart B-to-B marketers will find more and more ways to take advantage of this trend.

Another, even more powerful, reason? Video brings results. In widely cited statistics from Forrester Research, video increases the chance of a front page Google organic search engine result by 53 times. Adding video to emails increases click-through rates by two to three times. With numbers like those, video is the medium to watch.

10. Mobile Will Happen

Mobile is already happening. According to Gartner, Inc., a leading information technology research and advisory company, 1.6 billion mobile devices were sold in 2010. Smartphone sales grew 72 percent. An estimated 4.6 billion mobile phone subscriptions are held by 3.4 billion subscribers worldwide. Morgan Stanley analysts predict the Mobile Web will be bigger than desktop Internet use by 2015—with Gartner projecting mobile devices to overtake PCs as the most common web devices by 2013. That puts mobile into the "first screen" category—a customer's initial source of Internet information. No wonder Forrester Research predicts that B-to-B mobile marketing spending will quadruple by 2014, rising from $26 million in 2009 to $106 million.

It makes sense. Even while they're on the go, business professionals need—and increasingly expect—access to information in real time. Shipping giant FedEx's website now includes a category called "Mobile Shipping Solutions," which touts such business benefits as being able to "track while you travel" and "get rates from the golf course."

The integration of mobile technology into traditional media offers business marketers other unique opportunities—for instance, the ability to generate leads from print advertisements by adding mobile short codes and mobile barcodes.

Some industry experts predict that soon businesses will be expected to have a mobile site just as they are expected to have a traditional website today. According to the 2010 Pew Internet and American Life Project, 29 percent of mobile users already download apps that help their "productivity." In short, business marketers can create real value by thinking "upwardly mobile."

With trends like these on the horizon, the future of lead generation is a bright one. Now, let's go get the business.

Index

A

Aberdeen Group, 158, 161-162, 167

Accenture, banner ad targeting by domain name, 81

accounting systems, internal data, 37

acknowledgment page, lead nurturing, 161

activity-based measurements, tracking leads, 189

affinity groups, campaign target selection, 102

affinity marketing, future of, 194

Albee, Ardath, 148-149

allowable cost per lead, calculating, 27-30

AMD, marketing automation case study, 73-74

Anritsu, lead generation case study, 13-15

appended information, external data, 42-43

Armstrong, Stephen D., 195

assessing cost per lead by medium, 89

attention-getting words, 108

automated distribution lists, 155

Azulay, David, 90

B

banner ad targeting by domain name, 81

BANT (Budget, Authority, Need, Time frame), 140

behavioral data versus descriptive data, 34

benchmarketing lead-management processes, 155-156

benefits of lead nurturing, 158
campaign productivity, 158

best practices
B-to-B (business-to-business) marketing, 156
content marketing, 66-68

developing winning content, 68-69
resources, 70
data hygiene, 50
landing pages, 127-128
lead nurturing, 161-162
communications strategies, 162
content development, 163-164
marketing automation systems, 166-167
tracking, 164-165
triggered marketing, 165-166
managing campaign risk, 63, 64-65
marketing automation, 71-72
case studies, 73-74
vendors, 72-73
research and testing, 60
improving lead-generation results, 61-63
qualitative and quantitative pre-campaign research, 60-61

Birkhahn, Ted, 89

blogs, 88-89

Bly, Bob, 104

Brandon, Mary, 194-195

BRC (business reply card), 13

break-even campaign response rates, establishing, 30-31

broadcast advertising, 87

Brown, Michael A., 151

B-to-B (business-to-business) marketing, 5
  affinity marketing, 194
  banner ad targeting by domain name, 81
  lead generation, 77
    broadcast advertising, 87
    direct mail, 77-79
    email to cold prospects, 87
    outbound telemarketing, 77
    print advertising, 86
    search engine marketing, 80-81
    trade shows, 82-84
    websites, 82
  response rate benchmarks, 79

B-to-B segmentation variables, campaign target selection, 102-103

budgets, planning campaign budgets, 27
  calculating allowable cost per lead, 27-30
  establishing break-even campaign response rates, 30-31

business mailers, 80

business marketing databases, data fields, 47-48

business reply card (BRC), 13-14, 164

business reply envelope (BRE), 136

business target universes, 60

business-to-business. B-to-B (business-to-business) marketing *See* B-to-B

mailers, 51

buyers, 22
  relationships with sellers, 23-24
  technology buyers, changes in media preferences, 76

buying committees, 22
  motivating, 22

buying processes, 20-21, 23-24

C

calculating
  allowable cost per lead, campaign budgets, 27-30
  break-even campaign response rates, 30-31
  campaign volume requirements, 28
  conversations, lead flow planning, 25
  cost per lead by medium, 93
  lead requirements worksheet, lead flow planning, 25-26

campaign planning, objectives, 24-25

campaign productivity, lead nurturing, 158

campaign target selection, 102-
  B-to-B segmentation variables, 102-103
  platforms, 103-104

campaigns
  buying processes, 20-21
  calculating volume requirements, 28
  lead-generation campaigns, 20
  planning budgets, 27
    calculating allowable cost per lead, 27-30
    establishing break-even campaign response rates, 30-31

reaching the customer inside, 104-105

Cardbrowser, 193

case studies
  Anritsu, 13-15
  lead nurturing, 167-171
  marketing automation, 73-74

CHAID (Chi-Square Automatic Interaction Detector), 57

channel partner databases, data fields, 49

Chaplo, Mike, 96

classifying data, 34
  behavioral versus descriptive, 34
  customer versus prospect, 35
  internal versus external, 35-46

closed leads, 4

closed loop systems, tracking leads, 184-186

clustering, 57

CMI (ContentMarketingInstitute.com), 70

CMOs (chief marketing officers), challenges for, 1-2

cold inquiries, 74

communications strategies, lead nurturing, 162

Communispace, 92

compiled lists, 39-40

confidence levels, 63

content assets, 8

content development, lead nurturing, 163-164

content marketing, 8, 66-68
  developing winning content, 68-69
  future of, 70
  resources, 70

ContentMarketingInstitute.com (CMI), 70

contests, social networks, 92

control groups
    enterprise-wide, 65
    tracking leads, 188

conversations, calculating for lead flow planning, 25

conversion, 4

conversion rates, 4

converting, product features into customer benefits, 106

cooperative list development, LinkedIn, 91

copy, attention-getting words, 108

copywriters, getting best work from, 118-120

corporate energy executives, 21

cost per lead, 179-181

cost per lead by medium
    assessing, 89
    calculating, 93

creative work, getting best work from freelancers, 118-120

crediting sales, 189

criteria, for segmentation, 55-57

CRM (customer relationship management), 5

Cunningham, Valerie Mason, 185

customer benefits, converting product features into, 106

customer data versus prospect data, 35

customer relationship management (CRM), 5

customer service systems, internal data, 37-38

customer winback, 85

customers
    campaign target selection, 102-105
    defined, 3
    evolving behavior, 196

D

data, classifying, 34
    behavioral versus descriptive, 34
    customer versus prospect, 35
    internal versus external, 35-46

data capture, determining what data elements to capture, 129-130

data discovery, 44
    external data, 43-44

data fields, 46-49

data hygiene, 85
    best practices, 50
    processes, 51-54
    standardization, 51-52
    training, 52

data match-back, tracking leads, 187

decision-makers, 22

Demandbase, 45

descriptive data versus behavioral data, 34

design tips, lead generation, 109-110

developing winning content, 68-69

direct mail, 77-79

direct mail metrics, lead generation, 177

direct mail response rate benchmarks for business services, 179

direct mail response rate benchmarks for technology and manufacturing, 178

direct-response marketing, 5
    developing offers they can't refuse, 110-111

display advertising, 178

Drefahl, Andrew, 64

duplicates, inquiry fulfillment, 135

E

Eloqua, 149, 166

email, lead generation, 87

email lists, 42

email metrics, lead generation, 177

email response rate benchmarks for business services, 179

email response rate benchmarks for technology and manufacturing, 179

end-user sampling, tracking leads, 186-187

enterprise-wide control groups, 65

E:R (expense-to-revenue ratio), 183-184

events, qualifying leads, 150

exclusive offers, tracking leads, 188

expense-to-revenue ration (E:R), 183-184

external data, 38
    appended information, 42-43
    data discovery, 43-44
    email lists, 42
    internet-based data sources, 44-45
        Demandbase, 45
        Jigsaw, 44
        LinkedIn, 45
        ZoomInfo, 44-45
    prospect lists, 38-39
        compiled lists, 39-40
        response lists, 40-41
    prospecting databases, 41-42

F

face-to-face events, future of, 194-195

Fatino, Ann, 73

Flatley, Bill, 81

freelancers, lead generators, 118-120

fulfillment packages, 136

G

gatekeepers, 22

Gillett, J. T., 83

Gillin, Paul, 67

GlobalSpec, 66

Golec, Chris, 45

Google, 68

guided voice mail support, 85

H

Hacker Group, 64, 143

hard offers, 111

Hasbrouck, John, 96

headlines
creative checklist for, 110
landing pages, 128

Hebel, Bill, 92

hot leads, 74

I

Ideal, 11

improving lead-generation campaign results, 61-63

influencers, 22

information offers, 115-118

inquirers, 2

inquiries, scoring, 149

inquiry, defined, 3

inquiry files, internal data, 38

inquiry fulfillment, 132
capturing information according to source, 132-133
inquiry handling, 133-134
lead generation processes, 8
people involved in, 137
rules of, 134-136

inquiry generation, lead generation processes, 6-7

inquiry handling, 133-134

inquiry qualification, lead generation processes, 8-9

inquiry-to-lead conversion rate, 181-182

integrated marketing, multiple media, 95

internal data, 35
accounting systems, 37
customer service systems, 37-38
inquiry files, 38
operating and fulfillment systems, 37
sales contact files, 35-36
website data, 38

internet-based data sources, 44-45
Demandbase, 45
Jigsaw, 44
LinkedIn, 45
ZoomInfo, 44-45

J

Jigsaw, 44

K

keyword bidding, 80

King Industries, qualification criteria, 141

Klein, Mark, 63

Kourtis, Spyro, 80

L

Lail, Rob, 96

landing pages, 126-127
best practices, 127-128
determining what data elements to capture, 129-130
headlines, 128
number of, 128
placement counts, 130

Laverty, Dave, 167

lead flow planning, 25
calculating conversations, 25
calculating lead requirements worksheet, 25-26
tips for, 26-27

lead generation, 1, 3
B-to-B (business-to-business) marketing, 77
broadcast advertising, 87
direct mail, 77-79
email to cold prospects, 87
outbound telemarketing, 77
print advertising, 86
search engine marketing, 80-81
trade shows, 82-84
websites, 82
case studies, Anritsu, 13-15
direct mail metrics, 177
direct-response marketing, developing offers they can't refuse, 110-111
email metrics, 177
future of
affinity marketing, 194
evolving customer behavior, 196
face-to-face events, 194-195
marketing automation, 192
mobile technology, 197
new data sources for prospecting, 193
nurturing, 195-196
sales and marketing, 192
social media, 193-194
video, 196-197
headlines, creative checklist for, 110
market research for, 10-11
offers, matching to customer's buying processes, 114
organizational roles and responsibilities, 12

outbound lead generation
campaign media types,
97-99
PR, 84-85
processes, 6
inquiry fulfillment, 8
inquiry generation, 6-7
inquiry qualification, 8-9
lead nurturing, 9
lead tracking, 9-10
marketing automation,
71-72
response capture, 8
response planning, 7
referral marketing, 84
steps to success, 106-107
design tips, 109-110
what sells, 107-108
telephone-based, marketing
checkup, 151-153
types of offers, 113-114
Web 2.0, 88
blogs, 88-89
micro-blogging, 89
podcasts, 90-91
social networks, 91-92
syndication, 91
video, 89-90
webinars, 90
lead nurturing, 157
acknowledgment page, 161
benefits of, 158
campaign productivity,
158
best practices, 161-162
communications
strategies, 162
content development,
163-164
marketing automation
systems, 166-167
tracking, 164-165
triggered marketing,
165-166
case studies, 167-171
lead generation processes,
9
leader of, 159
media mix, 160-161
processes, 159-160
reasons companies don't
do it, 159

lead qualification, 140-141
BANT, 140
moving qualified leads into
pipeline, 142-143
secrets for success, 145
trade shows or events, 150
which leads to qualify,
143-145
lead requirements worksheet,
25-26
lead scoring, 146
based on website behavior,
148-149
improvement in campaign
results, 149
lead tracking, lead generation
processes, 9-10
lead-distribution decision
rules, 155
lead-generation campaign
results, improving, 61-63
lead-generation campaigns, 4-
5, 20
lead-ranking strategies, 145
lead scoring, 146
based on website
behavior, 148-149
sorting, 146
leads
automated distribution
lists, 155
benchmarketing lead-
management processes,
155-156
closed leads, 4
cold inquiries, 74
defined, 4
handing off to sales reps,
153-155
hot leads, 74
that don't close, 189
tracking, 184
activity-based
measurements, 189
closed-loop systems,
184-186
control groups, 188
data match-back, 187
end-user sampling,
186-187

exclusive offers, 188
product registration,
188-189
warm leads, 74
lead-to-sales conversion rates,
182-183
Lett, Stephen R., 65
LinkedIn, 45, 195
cooperative list
development, 91
live Internet chat, 85
look-alike prospects, 102

M

managing campaign risk,
63-65
market research, lead
generation, 10-11
Marketing 2.0, 167-171
marketing automation, 71-72
case studies, 73-74
future of, 192
vendors, 72-73
marketing automation
systems, 166-167
marketing checkup, telephone-
based lead generation,
151-153
marketing database (MDB), 34
data fields, 46-49
MarketingProfs.com, 70
Marketing Sherpa, 1, 21, 70,
156, 167
McFarlane, Hugh, 181
MDB. marketing database
(MDB) *See* measurement
rules, 185
media mix, 93-94
lead nurturing, 160-161
selecting, 92-93
media preferences, technology
buyers, changes in media
preferences, 76
metrics, 175-176, 181
cost per lead, 179-181
direct mail, 177

display advertising, 178
email metrics, 177
expense-to-revenue ration (E:R), 183-184
inquiry-to-lead conversion rate, 181-182
lead-to-sales conversion rates, 182-183
outbound telemarketing, 178
paid search metrics, 177
planning, 185
proxy metrics, 182
response rates, 176-179
micro-blogging, 89
mishandled response, 131-132
mobile technology, future of, 197
modeling, 57
motivating members of buying committees, 22
multiple media, 93-94
integrated marketing, 95

N

nurturing
defined, 4
future of, 195-196

O

Obermayer, Jim, 64, 137, 192, 196
objectives, for campaign planning, 24-25
offers
exclusive offers, 188
hard offers, 111
information, 115-118
matching to customer's buying processes, 114
retention offers, 112
soft offers, 111
Olivares, Denise, 194
operating and fulfillment systems, internal data, 37

organizational roles, for lead generation, 12
outbound lead generation campaign media types, 97-99
outbound telemarketing, 77, 178

P

paid search metrics, lead generation, 177
pay-per-click (PPC), landing pages, 128
personalization, inquiry fulfillment, 136
placement counts, landing pages, 130
planning metrics, 185
plant engineers, purchase decisions, 21
plant managers, purchase decisions, 21
platforms, campaign target selection, 103-104
players
buyers, 22
buying committees, 22
motivating, 22
decision-makers, 22
gatekeepers, 22
influencers, 22
in purchase decisions, 21
specifiers, 22
users, 22
Plexis Healthcare Systems, 83
podcasts, 90-91
Power Test, 64
PR, lead generation, 84-85
print advertising, 86
product features, converting into customer benefits, 106
product registration, tracking leads, 188-189
profiling, 57

promotions, social networks, 92
prospect data versus customer data, 35
prospect lists, 38-39
compiled lists, 39-40
response lists, 40-41
prospecting, new data sources for, 193
prospecting databases, external data, 41-42
prospects, defined, 3
proxy metrics, 182
purchase decisions, key players in, 21

Q

qualification criteria, 140-141
BANT (Budget, Authority, Need, Time frame), 140
moving qualified leads into pipeline, 142-143
questions to ask, 141-143
which leads to qualify, 143-145
qualification rates, 4
qualifications, 4-12
qualified leads, 4
qualifying leads, at trade shows or events, 150
qualitative pre-campaign research, 60-61
quantitative pre-campaign research, 60-61
questions to ask, for qualification criteria, 141-143

R

RainToday.com, 70
Rapp Collins, 120
referral marketing, lead generation, 84

referrals, social networks, 91

relevance rules, inquiry fulfillment, 135

Reneau, Robert, 182

research
best practices, 60
qualitative and quantitative pre-campaign research, 60-61
Google, 68
sources for, 66-67

resources, content marketing, 70

response capture, 124-126
lead generation processes, 8

response lists, 40-41

response management, 123-124
inquiry fulfillment, 132
capturing information according to source, 132-133
inquiry handling, 133-134
people involved in, 137
rules of, 134-136
landing pages, 126-127
best practices, 127-128
number of, 128
mishandled response, 131-132
processes, 124
response capture, 124-126

response planning, lead generation processes, 7

response rate benchmarks, B-to-B (business-to-business) marketing, 79

response rates, 3, 176-179

responsibilities for lead generation, 12

retention offers, 112

RightNow Technologies, 129

risk, managing, 63-65

Rule of 45, 157

S

Sao, Sham R., 45

sales, crediting, 189

sales and marketing, future of, 192

sales contact files, internal data, 35-36

sales reps, handing off leads to, 153-155

Sanderson, Oak, 73

scoring
inquiries, 149
webinar interactions, 149

search engine marketing (SEM), 80-81, 177

segmentation, 54-55
criteria for, 55-57

Sehringer, Gottfried, 184

selecting media mix, 92-93

sellers, relationships with buyers, 23-24

selling processes, 23-24

Sewell, Howard J., 161

Shea, Sean, 78

social media, future of, 193-194

social networks, lead generation, 91-92

soft offers, 111

sorting leads, 146

sources, for research, 66-67

specifiers, 22

speed, inquiry fulfillment, 134-135

standardization, data hygiene, 51-52

Stein, Lee Marc, 65

success in lead qualification, 145

syndication, 91

T

targeting, 54-55

technology buyers, changes in media preferences, 76

telemarketing, 77
power of, 85
voice mail marketing, 78-79

telephone-based lead generation, marketing checkup, 151-153

Tenenbaum, Linda, 156

testing
best practices, 60
improving lead-generation results, 61-63

Tooker, Richard N., 65

Totah, Dennis, 44

tracking
lead nurturing, 164-165
leads, 184
activity-based measurements, 189
closed-loop systems, 184-186
control groups, 188
data match-back, 187
end-user sampling, 186-187
exclusive offers, 188
product registration, 188-189
visitors to your site, 83

trade shows
lead generation, 82-84
qualifying leads, 150

training, data hygiene, 52

triggered marketing, lead nurturing, 165-166

types of offers, lead generation, 113-114

U

U.S. Postal Service (USPS), Business-to-Business mailers, 52

users, 22

V

Van Diepen, Katherine, 13

van Pelt, Marten G., 81

Vancil, Richard, 184

Veit, Michael, 90

vendors, marketing
   automation, 72-73

video
   future of, 196
   lead generation, 89-90

viral marketing, lead
   generation, 84

visitors, tracking visitors to
   your site, 83

VisitorTrack, 83

Vogel, Karen Breen, 87

voice mail, 96-99

voice mail marketing, 78-79

volume requirements,
   calculating for campaigns, 28

Vorias, Bill, 63

VP of manufacturing
   operations, purchase
   decisions, 21

W

Wallen, Jan, 193-194

warm leads, 74

Web 2.0, lead generation, 88
   blogs, 88-89
   micro-blogging, 89
   podcasts, 90-91
   social networks, 91-92
   syndication, 91
   video, 89-90
   webinars, 90

webinars, 90
   scoring interactions, 149

website data, internal data, 38

websites
   lead generation, B-to-B
      (business-to-business)
      marketing, 82
   lead scoring, 148-149
   tracking visitors, 83

WhichTestWon.com, 70

WIIFM (What's In It For
   Me?), 106

winning content, developing,
   68-69

Z

ZoomInfo, 44-45

Try Safari Books Online FREE
Get online access to 5,000+ Books and Videos

FREE TRIAL—GET STARTED TODAY!
www.informit.com/safaritrial

Find trusted answers, fast
Only Safari lets you search across thousands of best-selling books from the top technology publishers, including Addison-Wesley Professional, Cisco Press, O'Reilly, Prentice Hall, Que, and Sams.

Master the latest tools and techniques
In addition to gaining access to an incredible inventory of technical books, Safari's extensive collection of video tutorials lets you learn from the leading video training experts.

WAIT, THERE'S MORE!

Keep your competitive edge
With Rough Cuts, get access to the developing manuscript and be among the first to learn the newest technologies.

Stay current with emerging technologies
Short Cuts and Quick Reference Sheets are short, concise, focused content created to get you up-to-speed quickly on new and cutting-edge technologies.

QUE

quepublishing.com

Browse by Topic ▾ | Browse by Format ▾ | USING | More ▾

Store | Safari Books Online

QUEPUBLISHING.COM
Your Publisher for Home & Office Computing

Quepublishing.com includes all your favorite—
and some new—Que series and authors to help you
learn about computers and technology for the home,
office, and business.

Looking for tips and tricks, video tutorials, articles and
interviews, podcasts, and resources to make your life
easier? Visit **quepublishing.com**.

- **Read the latest articles and sample chapters**
  by Que's expert authors

- **Free podcasts** provide information on the
  hottest tech topics

- **Register your Que products** and receive updates,
  supplemental content, and a coupon to be used
  on your next purchase

- **Check out promotions and special offers**
  available from Que and our retail partners

- **Join the site** and receive members-only offers
  and benefits

Business Management

Finance and Investing

Graphics, Pictures & Video

Gadgets & Hardware

General Computing

Entertainment & Gaming

Internet & Web Apps

Computer Software

Operating Systems

Web Design & Development

QUE NEWSLETTER
quepublishing.com/newslette

 twitter.com/
quepublishing

 facebook.com/
quepublishing

 youtube.com/
quepublishing

 quepublishing.com/
rss

Que Publishing is a publishing imprint of Pearson

OWN OTHER GEEKY DEVICES? CHECK OUT THE MY...BOOK SERIES

ISBN 13: 9780789748263   ISBN 13: 9780789741165   ISBN 13: 9780789743039   ISBN 13: 9780789747150

Full-Color, Step-by-Step Guides

The "My..." series is a visually rich, task-based series to help you get up and running with your new device and technology and tap into some of the hidden, or less obvious features. The organized, task-based format allows you to quickly and easily find exactly the task you want to accomplish, and then shows you how to achieve it with minimal text and plenty of visual cues.

Visit quepublishing.com/mybooks to learn more about the My... book series from Que.

quepublishing.com

SOCIAL LOCATION MARKETING

Outshining Your Competitors on Foursquare, Gowalla, Yelp & Other Location Sharing Sites

SOCIAL MEDIA ROI

Managing and Measuring Social Media Efforts in Your Organization

OLIVIER BLANCHARD

BLOGGING TO DRIVE BUSINESS

Create and Maintain Valuable Customer Connections

ERIC BUTOW & REBECCA BOLLWITT

FACEBOOK MARKETING

THIRD EDITION

Designing Your Next Marketing Campaign

JUSTIN R. LEVY

Straightforward Strategies and Tactics for Business Today

The **Que Biz-Tech series** is designed for the legions of executives and marketers out there trying to come to grips with emerging technologies that can make or break their business. These books help the reader know what's important, what isn't, and provide deep inside know-how for entering the brave new world of business technology, covering topics such as mobile marketing, microblogging, and iPhone and iPad app marketing.

- Straightforward strategies and tactics for companies who are either using or will be using a new technology/product or way of thinking/ doing business

- Written by well-known industry experts in their respective fields— and designed to be an open platform for the author to teach a topic in the way he or she believes the audience will learn best

- Covers new technologies that companies must embrace to remain competitive in the marketplace and shows them how to maximize those technologies for profit

- Written with the marketing and business user in mind—these books meld solid technical know-how with corporate-savvy advice for improving the bottom line

Visit **quepublishing.com/biztech** to learn more about the **Que Biz-Tech series**

MAXIMIZING LEAD GENERATION

The Complete Guide for **B2B** Marketers

RUTH P. STEVENS

FREE Online Edition

Your purchase of *Maximizing Lead Generation* includes access to a free online edition for 45 days through the Safari Books Online subscription service. Nearly every Que book is available online through Safari Books Online, along with more than 5,000 other technical books and videos from publishers such as Addison-Wesley Professional, Cisco Press, Exam Cram, IBM Press, O'Reilly, Prentice Hall, and Sams.

SAFARI BOOKS ONLINE allows you to search for a specific answer, cut and paste code, download chapters, and stay current with emerging technologies.

Activate your FREE Online Edition at
www.informit.com/safarifree

> **STEP 1:**   Enter the coupon code: ONUYKCB.

> **STEP 2:**   New Safari users, complete the brief registration form.
>   Safari subscribers, just log in.

If you have difficulty registering on Safari or accessing the online edition, please e-mail customer-service@safaribooksonline.com

Safari
Books Online

     Cisco Press   IBM Press   Microsoft Press   New Riders

O'REILLY Peachpit Press PRENTICE HALL Que Redbooks SAMS SAS Sun WILEY